THE SECRETS OF WOMEN WHO NEVER GIVE UP

11 RESILIENCE-BUILDING STRATEGIES LEARNED FROM REMARKABLE WOMEN IN HISTORY

DR. KATJA LINDEMANN MD

CONTENTS

INTRODUCTION

When the student is ready the teacher will appear. When the student is truly ready... The teacher will disappear. –Tao Te Ching

I believe it is not a coincidence that you are holding this book at this very moment. Perhaps you were searching for an answer, guided by a higher power—or your own religious or spiritual understanding—or by an inner voice seeking support. There might be small challenges you wish to tackle or one overarching dilemma that you wish to resolve. Maybe this is your first time reading these paragraphs, or you might be returning in the hope of discovering a solution to a different problem.

In this book, you will learn about remarkable women in the past whose stories of success will teach you the secrets to never giving up in the *present*. The following pages contain 11 strategies designed to help you build resilience and inner strength so you can triumph over trials and tribulations to live a healthier and happier life. Each strategy has been extracted from the tried-and-tested approaches that were used by the women in this book; they have become mentors as their wisdom travels through time and is still relevant to us today.

This book has been designed for diverse readers facing particular challenges in different contexts, meaning that not all the strategies will be relevant to you at this point in your life. I have structured the book in such a way that it can either be read from start to finish as a historical account or as stand-alone chapters that can be easily referred to when necessary. However, I encourage you to read all the chapters in order, as every strategy is connected to all the others. I also encourage you to return to these pages whenever it might suit you, for what you might not have needed before may be exactly what you need now; take what strikes a chord and leave what does not.

Sometimes merely being aware of a specific strategy is sufficient. Other times, a combination of strategies might prove more useful. There are no set rules or instructions as to how the information should be interpreted. I have done my best to present this as a positive manifesto, even when talking about difficult subjects.

STORIES AND STRATEGIES OF SUCCESSFUL WOMEN

All the water in the world cannot drown you unless it gets inside of you. – Eleanor Roosevelt

The Story Behind the Book

In my life, much like everyone else, I have encountered difficult situations whose causes were often beyond my control. Unexpected challenges can arrive without warning, and curveballs get thrown out of the blue. I am certain that all of us have felt as if we have been—and will be—thrown into the deep end. But instead of allowing ourselves to drown, we have the option to stay afloat. Sometimes all we need is a little nudge in the right direction, reminding us that it is we who get to decide whether to sink or swim.

Despite tough times, I have somehow always found the strength inside myself to push through, determined to keep going. Over time, I developed a sense of direction and purpose that guided me where I needed to go. I am grateful to have always been surrounded by friends and family who supported me no matter what. Yet despite my strong connections with all the women in my life, I still had a deep longing for female mentors who could teach me how to overcome obstacles big and small through their extraordinary strength and wisdom. Later, I discovered that my female friends and family shared this longing for female mentorship, so I embarked on a journey of discovery that eventually led to this book's writing.

As a history lover, it was not uncommon for me to quiz my family and friends on their historical knowledge. I started asking questions and engaging in countless conversations with the people in my life. One question, in particular, was the spark that ignited the main idea behind this book. I asked those who were closest to me to name three remarkable women in history off the top of their heads and explain why these women were considered special. The responses I received utterly surprised me!

The majority of my female friends and family members could immediately name at least three women in history and could tell me what these women had achieved that made them remarkable. Some needed time to think it over but eventually came up with at least three names and had at least an idea of their achievements. Only a handful of my female friends had found a deeper significance in these women's stories, which they actively applied in their daily lives in pursuit of their achievements.

Interestingly, not a single one of my male friends could name even one remarkable woman in history. I wondered why this was—did I need new male friends? Just kidding! I could see that their lack of awareness was not their fault, as the realization made most of them either giggle nervously or squirm from embarrassment. Was it school that taught them to leave women in the shadows of history? Or was it society that conditioned them to only remember great men while the equally-as-great women remained in the background?

Upon deeper reflection, this was hardly surprising. In the Western world, true gender equality only emerged about 50 years ago. It is easy to forget that our grandmothers and mothers probably did not enjoy the modern liberties many of us take for granted and were expected to cook, clean, and raise children while the men left their homes to work. To this day, many countries still do not recognize women and men as equals; as a woman, I would not be allowed to write this book, for example.

History is no different, especially considering that the past was a time far more patriarchal than the present. Women were, for the most part, excluded from the historical narrative, and the ones who did make it into the books were exceptions. I started compiling a list of these exceptional women, trying to find out as much as I could, but my research revealed that historical data was scarce, patchy, and obscured in books that were few and far between.

Luckily, the internet is a treasure trove of information that was not accessible just two decades ago. From various sites and sources, I slowly pieced together a bigger picture, and what I had been seeking all along gradually emerged: These were the female mentors I had been searching for! The more I read their biographies, the more their stories invoked an emotional connection within me. Their journeys were not filled with struggles but revealed secrets that led to their success. Each woman's story was about overcoming obstacles against all odds, woven together by a common thread: The strengthening of resilience in the face of adversity.

A Personal Experience on Surrender: How I Used the Strategies Unaware of Their Resilience-Building Nature

Receiving the envelope that Tuesday afternoon made my heart sink. A letter from the College of Specialist Psychiatrists with the exam results telling me whether I had passed or not. This exam would determine if I was granted a fellowship with the College, which was crucial for the process of registration as a Medical Specialist Practitioner. The fellowship would allow my visa status to be changed to permanent residency. Most importantly, it would end the dependency on employer sponsorship in the hospital system.

A brittle system only held together by amazing individuals who are unable to speak up about its issues. One of the main issues is the arrangement of absolute career dependency for international medical graduates, and this, in turn, is tied to dependency on the goodwill of the employer.

I held on to my dog, too scared to open the letter by myself; my hands were shaking. It did not sound like a life-threatening situation, and it was irrational to be so frightened, but at that moment, I felt everything as if my whole life depended on it. I opened the letter and started reading. The beginning of the letter did not sound promising, and below the first lines, there it was: *failed*. Written in capital letters, impossible to miss.

My world came crashing down. All the hard work, months of studying, preparation, and sacrifice were instantly rendered useless. I missed so many important events in my step-children's (I like to lovingly call them my "bonus-children") lives: school assemblies, soccer games, football finals, and many more. Just having the headspace and being receptive to their lives' worries was not something I could do as much as I would have liked. It made me feel guilty as I was either at work, unable to take time off, on-call doing the rounds on the ward, or studying and attending training programs while navigating my elderly and sick parents' needs on the other side of the world without any other familial support. There was not much time for anything else in my life.

Failed. Luckily, my dog was prepared to catch the tears running down my face. I felt so disappointed, frustrated, and overwhelmed. Thoughts were racing through my head, and I started to panic, thinking about the fellowship. Even though I already hold Specialist registration in a different country, I would not be able to get the registration where I lived. That had been the last chance to sit the exam, as the College was changing to a new system, and it was clearly stated that they would not carry on with candidates who had not completed the requirements. I was getting desperate.

I don't want to leave the country, was my only thought. My beautiful Kelpie dog, with her friendly and joyful face, was happy to be held close, allowing me to hide more of my tears in her dusty fur. "I don't want this to be the end. It can't be the end," but reality showed that this was, indeed, the end. I had better start packing my bags and getting ready to leave my life behind and the country I love and call home, where I have all my social connections.

For some weeks, I operated on autopilot and ignored the exam outcome as if it had not happened. I go to work, do my duties, get the groceries, cook dinner, and go to bed. Repeat day after day. I felt like giving up and running away to start again somewhere else, but there was a quiet voice inside me telling me that there is always another way. Initially, I argued with this voice, saying that there is not any other chance and that I already had a Specialist degree; why couldn't it just be accepted by the College, and why was the system so unsupportive and unfair? What bad things have I done to deserve these struggles? Why can't I just enjoy life like other people? I was angry with the system, the people in charge, and the world, unable to accept that it was my shortcomings that led me to this point.

That soft and quiet voice inside me did not give up; it was telling me the same thing over and over again "There is always another way." I somehow started to listen and continued to put one foot in front of the other. I had not come this far to just give up at this stage. I knew that there was a purpose for my skills. I started to remember why I had chosen this profession. Why did I put all this effort and training into it? What was driving me to start this journey? I remembered the night I made the decision to become a Medical Doctor.

It was a Friday evening during my last year of school. I happened to watch an elderly lady fall from a chair in the restaurant. Most people were just staring at the situation, not knowing what to do, except for one man who stood up, calmly approached her, and managed the emergency with ease. It turned out that he was a Medical Doctor, one of the local General Practitioners. He was managing the situation with such competence that his approach really moved me. It was at that moment that I decided to enroll in medical school, wanting to know what he knew and conduct myself like him in situations like this. Being able to manage health crises has been my drive for more than two decades.

The memory of my *why* came back; this was a turning moment. I was not going to give up, but I realized I could not do it on my own. I reached out to a mentor who would support me over the coming months, getting my feet back on the ground.

Meanwhile, I found the courage to honestly talk to my employer about the failed exam and expressed that I would need further support to continue. I was granted another sponsorship visa by my employer. More of the same dependency, but now, with the support of people around me, at least I could stay in the country I loved. In addition to that, I successfully applied for the College to grant me an exemption to sit for exams again. I was granted a retry, but the College also imposed an additional two years of training requirements on me. Even though these additional two years of training felt like punishment for failing the exam, I was not going to waste it; this was another chance.

I started to realize that I failed the exam because I could not demonstrate my competencies well enough. I knew I had skills but failed to show them. I began to understand that failure was part of the process and part of the path to success. It was there to help me get better at what I do. I was able to forgive myself for failing and be compassionate about my shortcomings. There was a shift in my thinking, from a low point of anger and feeling that "the world is against me and I'm never going to get there," to a point where I was grateful for another opportunity; where I wanted to learn more and to do things in a better way, not just pass the exams but to become a better doctor for my patients. It was not just about me and my visa anymore; it was about something greater than that. The exam suddenly shrank to a small obstacle, and I had a clear pathway in front of me where every step seemed achievable.

It was only after this mental shift that I was able to honestly look deep inside at my deficiencies. With the support of my mentor and my new passionate approach, I was able to work on the shortcomings that had led to my failing the exam the first time. I had a clear vision and a strong belief in my *why*, combined with a great reason to succeed. The exam was initially a big hurdle, but as it turned out, forgetting the purpose I envisioned that day as a teen actually made the obstacle insurmountable.

Some Definitions of Resilience

The meaning of resilience is multifaceted and depends on the context in which it is defined. Put simply; resilience means recovering quickly from difficulties. This book makes a distinction between physical and psychological resilience as two different sides of the same coin, as follows:

- Physical resilience: Or elasticity, is the ability of something to bounce back to its original shape after a disturbance and can be understood as flexibility (as opposed to rigidity). Ecological resilience, for instance, is the capacity of an ecosystem (such as soil or climate) to quickly recover to its natural state after a natural disaster.
- Psychological resilience: An individual's capacity to cope emotionally and mentally when faced with a crisis or tragedy and is akin to someone's strength of character (in contrast to vulnerability).

In this book, we will focus on the latter definition.

According to the American Psychological Association (APA) in the Dictionary of Psychology (2022):

Resilience: "The process and outcome of successfully adapting to difficult or challenging life experiences, especially through mental, emotional, and behavioral flexibility and adjustment to external and internal demands. Several factors contribute to how well people adapt to adversities, predominant among them being (a) how individuals view and engage with the world, (b) the availability and quality of social resources, and (c) specific coping strategies. Psychological research demonstrates that the resources and skills associated with more positive adaptation (i.e., greater resilience) can be cultivated and practiced. Also called psychological resilience."

Resilience is important to humans in general, as it ensures the survival of the human race while also having cultural and historical significance in teaching us about ourselves.

Cultural resilience is the ability to deal with and overcome adversity not individually but with the support of a community with a common cultural background. Cultural resilience characterizes adaptability in the face of adversity as a dynamic, rather than static, process influenced by the external environment.

With all that information and definitions, let us get to the point: How do we become more resilient? With this book, we only intend to give tools to answer this apparently simple question.

ACKNOWLEDGING OUR BELIEFS AND FAITH

Why do you pray, if you doubt you are heard? –Alexandra David-Néel

INTRODUCTION

L et me ask you one important question: What is it you believe in? Or before you start pondering the answer, a more pertinent question would be: Is there something you believe in? Something greater than us all? Maybe in something closer to our plane: Do you believe in yourself? In the path you lay out for yourself? In your ability to go down that path with or without support?

All of these questions and their respective answers are the first steps on the path toward faith. Understanding what you believe in resolves the most fundamental questions in your life: What is the meaning behind my existence? What is our purpose? What did I come here to do? And once you arrive at the answer, can you attach your faith to that new-found truth?

The rules-defying woman whose life is barely sketched in this chapter is an example of unyielding faith, with its highs and lows, but with her truth never put into question.

Belief and Faith: Definitions

Perhaps we should agree on definitions first. Let us go to our trusted dictionaries for answers. Merriam-Webster (2019) tells us about belief:

- "A state or habit of mind in which trust or confidence is placed in some person or thing."
- "Something that is accepted, considered to be true, or held as an opinion: something believed. Especially: a tenet or body of tenets held by a group."
- "Conviction of the truth of some statement or the reality of some being or phenomenon, especially when based on examination of evidence."

In these three definitions, we can find two types of beliefs: Those of a group and those of individuals. Do not lose sight of this distinction, as we will discuss it later in this chapter.

From a more pertinent source, the APA Dictionary (n.d.), belief:

- "Acceptance of the truth, reality, or validity of something (e.g., a phenomenon, a person's veracity), particularly in the absence of substantiation."
- "An association of some characteristic or attribute, usually evaluative in nature, with an attitude object (e.g., this car is reliable)."

Now we extract the meaning of faith from the same sources. From Merriam-Webster (2011):

"Allegiance to duty or a person: loyalty."
"Fidelity to one's promises."
"Sincerity of intentions."

2

"Belief and trust in and loyalty to God."
"Belief in the traditional doctrines of a religion."

"Firm belief in something for which there is no proof."
"Complete trust."
"Something that is believed, especially with strong conviction."

For Merriam-Webster, we can clearly see another important distinction between belief and faith. The former implies trust in something that has material proof, while the latter implies trust in something that does not have material proof. This distinction may prove useful later.

The definition from the APA Dictionary (n.d.-b) for faith is:

"Unwavering loyalty, belief, and trust."

For context, the word faith is derived from the Latin *fides*, a deity, and the Roman pagan goddess of trust and good faith (bona fides), one of the original divine virtues. *Fides* is also the root of the word fidelity, which understands this as a sense of duty to be loyal and faithful to oneself and others.

Finally, in philosophy, a belief is a "propositional attitude." It is the attitude we take when we regard a statement as true. We can define it as a mental state we are in when we have a stance, opinion, or take about a proposition or the potential state of affairs in which a proposition is true.

A WOMAN WHO BELIEVED AND HAD FAITH

Alexandra David-Néel: Forbidden to Lose Faith

The story of Alexandra David-Néel should start by stating that she lived to the age of 101. A little over a century to live, learn, and teach. She was born Louise Eugénie Alexandrine Marie David in Paris on October 24, 1868. Just to give some perspective, she lived through the Paris Commune, both World Wars, the foundation of the People's Republic of China, and even the first Woodstock. At the beginning of her life, she was being transported around the *merveilleuse* Paris in a carriage pulled by horses—exactly like those in the movies—and lived long enough to see the advent of the car, even being the owner of one herself.

The library of her father was the place where Alexandra would spend hours and days of her childhood reading Jules Verne's adventures and philosophical treatises. She received the standard education most *bourgeoises* families at the time gave their daughters: rigid and religious. Among the disciplines she studied was classical singing, a subject that would prove important later in her life. Her father and mother were like day and night, one a Socialist journalist (protestant and Freemason), and the other a Belgian devoted Roman Catholic (with an interest in investments) and wife.

At eighteen, she took her bicycle and set out to pedal across Europe, an adventure unheard of for a girl at the time. Three years later, visiting the Guimet Museum, the young Alexandra found what she did not know she was looking for; a giant statue of Buddha that would change her vision of the world forever.

Her fantasies of visiting India were made possible only a little while later, in 1890, thanks to the inheritance her grandmother left. But this money would only last for a year, a situation that made Alexandra accept a position as singer for the Hanoi Theater's Opera House in Indochina. She then went on a *tournée* through the East, Greece, and Tunisia, among other places.

Tunisia was where she met Philippe Néel, an engineer working on a big project for the French government's railway construction. They lived together as lovers for four years, at the end of which he asked her to marry him. She was not very keen on marriage, though, and a letter was the method she chose to let him know that life as a wife and mother was not for her, but to no avail. They got married on October 4, 1904, at the consulate in Tunisia.

Life as a married woman brought many difficulties for Alexandra—as she had already anticipated—and the trips to the desert and on her husband's sailing boat were not enough. She loved Philippe, but the life he was offering her was not enough to make her happy. He was aware of this and arranged an educational *voyage* to India with the Ministry of Education. She departed on August 9, 1911. The plan was for her to return after 18 months. She returned 14 years later.

In the first couple of years, Alexandra traveled across the country, and by 1912, she had reached Nepal. Later, Sikkim, a state in India situated in the Himalayas. There, she met her soon-to-be life companion, the only one who accompanied her on all her travels, Aphur Yongden. The boy was 14 years old at the time. When they arrived at Kalimpong, she heard from the locals that the sovereign of Tibet, the 13th Dalai Lama, was exiled there; his country was at war with China. She made it her mission to visit him, even though he refused to meet with foreign women. After much insistence, he finally gave in. For the meeting, Alexandra brought a *khata*—a white scarf symbolizing purity and compassion—as a good omen and respectfully presented it to him with a bow. Their conversation was the spark that lit her desire to uncover the secrets of Tibet. After their meeting, she would continue to study Buddhism and gather the resolution to travel to Lhasa.

In May of the same year, she and Yongden entered a Buddhist monastery located in a cave 4000 meters high in the Himalayan mountains. There, she would meditate, study religious doctrine, and exercise the Yogi practices. Her whole worldview changed; she had nothing and was living on the charity of other monks. Relinquishing all material goods was fundamental to reaching religious enlightenment. She stayed at the monastery for two and a half years. At the end of her time there, the monks named her "Lamp of Wisdom" and Yongden "Ocean of Peace."

The 18 months originally planned for her journey were long gone. It was 1916, and without permission from the authorities, she entered Tibet for the first time. Unfortunately, she got caught, and the English governor threatened her with deportation if she did not return to India. At the time, Tibet was a forbidden place for foreigners; neither the English nor the Chinese wanted outsiders there. A bit discouraged, she continued her travels and, eventually, arrived in Japan, where Ekai Kawaguchi—a philosopher and monk she encountered— explained how he had managed to live for a year and a half in Lhasa without being discovered. The secret was to pass off as a Chinese monk. She resolved then and there that she would do the same.

It was October 1923 when the opportunity arrived. To divert attention, Alexandra and Yongden told everyone they were leaving for the mountains to collect medicinal herbs. She disguised herself as a pilgrim beggar and the young man as her Lama's son. With cacao ashes to darken her complexion and yak tail hair dyed with ink, braided in the customs of the Tibetan women as a wig, she would act as the widow of a Lama.

They carried backpacks with just enough to survive, as they would make their journey on foot. When they reached the mountains, it dawned on them what an odyssey they were about to go through. With the Mekong River as a guide, they faced innumerable dangers: thieves, pilgrims who could find out she was a foreigner, checkpoints, the awful terrain, precipices, the swellings of the river, snow, and ice. The food was scarce, and they would have fevers often. In order to go unnoticed, they would travel by night, taking alternative routes. Sometimes they came across villages, and those were the best days. But there were the worst days as well: They starved for days and came close to freezing to death. Extreme exhaustion could only be overcome by meditating.

The last few weeks were the most difficult. Yongden broke an ankle, and they had to stop for several days without food or sleep. But against all odds, they continued on their path until Lhasa finally presented itself to them in the shape of the Potala Palace, the palace of the Dalai Lamas. A majestic view of golden roofs and red and white walls. The journey lasted eight months. Their arrival coincided with the Buddhist New Year, and they were lucky enough for a kind woman to offer food and accommodation. Alexandra had, at last, fulfilled her dream.

They stayed in Lhasa for four months without anyone noticing who she was. On May 10, 1925, Alexandra and Yongden arrived at Le Havre. Phillippe was there to welcome them. He agreed, and the couple adopted Yongden as their legitimate son four years later.

She spent her remaining years—many of them—traveling, teaching, and writing about Buddhism, Hinduism, and Taoism. Upon Alexandra's death, her ashes were scattered in the Ganges River, as she had desired. And she will undoubtedly be remembered as an adventurer and the first woman to ever visit Tibet.

IMPLEMENTING BELIEF AND FAITH INTO A STRATEGY FOR RESILIENCE

Believing in Our Own Truth Versus Focusing on Facts

Alexandra taught us that achieving a dream is a matter of not giving up. She deeply believed in herself and had the conviction that she would get to Lhasa, even though everything around her pointed to the opposite. It was a path of great difficulty, but it was one she willingly took.

No foreigners were allowed in Tibet; that was a certainty.

And despite being aware of the rules, she chose to pursue her dream regardless. To some, this conviction might have looked like an obsession. And maybe it was; on closer examination, it was the drive she needed to achieve her goal of seeing and breathing Lhasa.

None of the obstacles or setbacks Alexandra experienced were enough to make her lose her belief. She chose to listen to her truth—to have faith—instead of focusing on the hard facts. These facts were very apparent:

The first big obstacle she had to overcome was what her time and culture expected of her. A woman traveling alone was something unfit for her contemporaries' closed minds. Moreover, a married woman was supposed to be a good wife and look after the children. She instead followed her calling and faith.

The second big obstacle was the negative response of the authorities to her request to go to Lhasa and the threat of deportation.

The third main obstacle was the cold and the immensity of those mountains. And perhaps the naiveté with which they faced the challenge.

Alexandra's leitmotif was that one's choice of not listening to our faith results in losing our ability to be resilient in the hardest moments. She even went a step further and said, "Suffering raises up those soils that are truly great; it is only small souls that are made mean-spirited by it" (David-Néel, n.d.). Teaching even further, "The only truth which is living and effective, which is of value, is the truth which we ourselves discover" (David-Néel & Yongden, 1967, p. 13).

She is one of many examples where the mantra "we become what we believe" turns into reality. She had the unshakable belief that she could fulfill her dream of getting to Lhasa. She believed it so strongly that she acted as if she were already there; she darkened her skin and wore the traditional clothes of a woman in Lhasa. Despite all the obstacles and barriers, she became a woman in Lhasa because she believed in it.

We can learn and embrace the faith taught by others—that is, a *collective* faith—and she certainly did when she isolated herself in that cave and practiced Buddhism. But at the same time, she had her *individual* faith: in her journey to self-realization and a destiny.

What we can take from her is that whether you choose—or are chosen by a higher power—to follow a collective faith, your individual faith, or both of them, the fact is that they are there to guide and show you your purpose amid turbulence. Do not waste your faith.

To finish, Professor Brené Brown teaches us about faith: "Faith is a place of mystery where we find the courage to believe in what we cannot see and the strength to let go of our fear of uncertainty." And "Faith is essential when we decide to live and love with our whole hearts in a world where most of us want assurances before we risk being vulnerable and getting hurt. To say, "I'm going to engage wholeheartedly in my life requires believing without seeing" (2010, p. 63).

But this is not about what we cannot see; it is about what we can only see with our inner eye. It is not there in the material world yet, but it is visible to us inside. Probably one of the most quoted sets of words in history adds to that "It is only with the heart that one can see rightly; what is essential is invisible to the eye" (Saint-Exupéry, 1943, p. 74).

An Invitation for Reflection to Find Your Faith and a Call to Action to Grow Resilience

Find a notebook or journal and complete the following exercise: Listen to your inner voice telling you the *truth* and answer some questions:

- What would you do if there were no limiting beliefs, and you knew you could not fail?
- What journey would you take if you had faith in yourself and believed in the greatness in you?
- What choices would you make if you found your faith?
- Do you let others *talk you out of it*? And do you let others determine what you can or cannot do?
- Do you let your doubts take over your ideas and dreams? It is only when we stop doubting that we begin to believe in our new life—the life of our dreams.
- Create some affirmations and read them to yourself every day for at least 21 days. E.g.:
- Following my faith in myself and the guidance of the higher powers comes naturally to me.
- I choose faith over fear and doubt.

2

DEFINING OUR VALUES

Each person must live their life as a model for others. –Rosa Parks

INTRODUCTION

We, as social animals, need rules to live among each other and within ourselves. Many of the rules we now view as intrinsic to our societies have historically come from religions. The rules in us are called values, and we often choose them according to our environments and personalities. Building on our previous strategy, this chapter will address what happens when people lose their values by telling the stories of two women who held theirs tightly and one who lost some along the way. But all of them changed the world for the better.

What Values Are

For values, we have the following broad definition from our trusted APA Dictionary (n.d.), and leaving aside the obvious definitions for the fields of mathematics and economics, we can quote:

"A moral, social, or aesthetic principle accepted by an individual or society as a guide to what is good, desirable, or important" (para. 2)

And the origin of the word can be traced to being derived from Old French, being the feminine past participle of the word *valoir* meaning "be worth," and this, in turn, is from the Latin word *valere*.

Now let us dive deeper into the concepts of value in the fields of ethics and the social sciences.

Values are a guide to how it is best to live and how it is best to act when we face a particular event. They are a sort of scale to help us decide the degree of importance—and the meaning—some actions or things have compared to others. One of the most important aspects of the concept is that values can change over time.

The distinction between personal values and cultural values that exist in relation to one another—that is to say, one cannot exist without the other—will agree with, or diverge from, societal written norms:

Personal values provide us with an internal reference—a moral compass—of what is good, beneficial, desirable, and important in our lives—a sense of right and wrong. In Western philosophy, values—along with needs, interests, and habits—are what influence behavior and the choices made by an individual. People express their individual values in daily life, and then these become the basis for law, custom, and tradition.

Cultural values are global abstract concepts compared to the norms of a particular culture; whereas norms are specific rules to follow in certain situations, values identify what should be judged as good or evil. It is not uncommon for personal and cultural values to be in conflict, which usually creates a subculture that differs from the mainstream. Non-conformity to the dominant cultural values can result in stigmatization and discrimination by others, and in some countries, it is punishable by law.

Personal values are often learned from parents through socialization, and the already-established cultural values that exist, which, as history illustrates, are constantly in flux.

Value systems are set beliefs that serve the purpose of ethical or ideological integrity and are both prospective—concerned with the future—and prescriptive (established as custom).

THREE WOMEN'S TEACHINGS ON VALUES

Rosa Parks: Standing Up by Sitting Down

Born on February 4, 1913, in Tuskegee, Alabama, Rosa Louise McCauley Parks became a heroine almost by accident. Her family was composed of her parents, Leona and James, and her younger brother, Sylvester. The context was an utterly racist one under the South's Jim Crow segregation laws, which forced black and white people to live in separate spaces.

When Rosa was two years old, her parent's business went bankrupt, and her father left the family. This forced them to move to her grandparents' home in Pine Level, arriving just in time for the Ku Klux Klan (KKK) to become active again. During those years, she would see her grandfather sit on the porch with a loaded shotgun during the parades of the KKK, fearing something might happen. People of color—especially black people—were being lynched and burned in the thousands in public spaces, almost as entertainment.

Education was very important in Rosa's family, but after changing schools a few times for different reasons, she was forced to drop out and find a job as a seamstress to take care of her mother and grandmother.

In 1932, she met dashing barber Raymond Park. He was a well-informed and proactive political subject. For someone like

Rosa, coming from the family she came from, he was the perfect match—so perfect that he proposed on their second date. But the politics were becoming more and more dangerous in the months after their wedding, and Raymond, fearing for her life, forbade her from attending the same meetings he did.

By 1933, she had finally earned her high school diploma, which allowed her to access a wider range of jobs. One of those was at Maxwell Air Force Base in Montgomery, where segregation laws did not apply. It was another world to her, and the experience planted the seed in her mind of what could be outside as well.

But ten years had to pass for Rosa to get closer to political activism. She and Raymond joined the Montgomery chapter of the National Association for the Advancement of Colored People (NAACP) to work as volunteers. Her tasks included writing records of racist violence to send to the media. This made her a known activist across the state. The following years were marked by increased tensions across many of the Southern states; the movement only needed a spark to set the fire.

That spark came on December 1, 1955. On her way home from work—she was working at a department store by that time —she took the bus as always and sat in the middle section, in the non-designated seats. The bus then filled with passengers, leaving a few standing. Seeing this, the driver, James F. Blake, demanded she and three other black passengers vacate the seats in favor of the white passengers, to which she was the only one to refuse. This action led to her arrest and a night in a cell for civil disobedience.

The defiance that day came from a woman, a black person, and a political activist, and this idea is essential because her political action and symbolism were later undermined, alleging her refusal to stand up came from tiredness. In her own words, "I was not tired physically, or no more tired than I usually was at the end of a working day. I was not old, although some people had an image of me as being old then. I was forty-two. No, the only tired I was was tired of giving in" (1992, p. 82).

That day was a turning point for the movement for civil rights. Other people felt inspired—Martin Luther King Jr. among them—and began a massive boycott of the segregation laws aboard Alabama buses, an action that lasted for over a year.

But life became harder for Rosa and her family after that; she was fired from her job, and people avoided her for being a *troublemaker*. They received death threats, and all sorts of fake news was spread about them. Despite this, she still advocated for a non-violent approach; "Nothing could be gained by violence, threats, or a belligerent attitude; we believe more could be accomplished through a non-violent passive resistance" (Rogers, 1955).

The law was finally overturned on December 20, 1956. But the threats continued, and jobs were scarce; the family moved to Michigan a year later for better economic prospects. Rosa was suffering from throat cancer, and until an article came out detailing her situation, the NAACP did not bother to help her in any way. From that moment on, the family began to improve its economic prospects.

Raymond would pass away in 1977, and Rosa would spend the rest of her life involved in politics, as she had always done.

She died as a symbol of resistance and fighting for justice on October 24, 2005, with her last remains placed on the Capitol for people to pay their respects.

Eleanor Roosevelt: From Privileged to Helping the Marginalized

Anna Eleanor Roosevelt was born on October 11th, 1884, in Manhattan, New York City. Curiously, her last name would remain the same until her death. Her parents were Elliot Roosevelt and Anna Rebecca Hall; the couple belonged to New York's high society, a situation that made her come into the world with immense wealth and privilege. Proof of this was that, through her father, she was a niece of President Theodore Roosevelt, among other famous people; besides her parents and herself, her family was completed with her two siblings. While her father was the loving figure in her life, her mother did not care much for her as she did not seem to meet her *high standards*.

Nevertheless, death seemed to follow her. At the age of eight, diphtheria took her mother and her brother, Elliot Jr., only a few months later. Her father Elliot had been an alcoholic for many years, and even though this did not prevent him from going on hunting trips in Africa or playing polo—with the occasional seasons in what we now call rehabilitation clinics—what would definitely bring him down was the laudanum and morphine added to the drinks he began consuming after an ankle fracture in 1893. While confined to a mental hospital, he jumped through a window during a delusional episode caused by withdrawal symptoms. He survived the fall but died later during a seizure.

After the tragedy, both she and her brother Hall were raised in her maternal grandmother's home. Even though their material needs were covered, Eleanor grew up insecure around others. She was home-schooled until her 15th birthday and later sent—at her aunt Anna's insistence—to Allenswood Academy, a private institution in London, England. The French headmistress, Marie Souvestre, became like a guardian and guide to Eleanor and helped her overcome many of her insecurities. Her relationship with the French language was special. She completed her education there in 1902 and returned to New York at the request of her grandmother.

That same year, Eleanor was presented to society at a ball at the Waldorf-Astoria Hotel and continued to lead a very social life. Her political inquisitiveness made her join several organizations. One of these was the National Consumers League, an organization that sought to defend workers' rights and advocated for people to buy goods manufactured by companies where there was no child exploitation.

Not long after, she met—for the second time—another Roosevelt, a cousin of her father named Franklin Delano. A little romance and correspondence were all it took for them to get engaged. Frank's mother, Sara, opposed the union but could not prevent it from taking place. And so, they got married on March 17, 1905, with President Theodore Roosevelt as the bride's companion.

During the next decade, she would commit—almost reluctantly—to motherhood and give birth to six children: Anna, James, Franklin Delano Jr.—who died a month after his birth—Eliott, another boy named Franklin Delano Jr., and John. But everyday life was hard with her mother-in-law living next door and controlling every aspect of Eleanor's home, from the everyday tasks to the children's upbringing, and criticizing her constantly.

In 1911, Franklin was elected to the Senate as a representative for New York, and the family moved to Albany. Eleanor had the opportunity to immerse herself in politics again by participating in organizations, as she did before they got married. Three years later, when the First World War broke out, she entered the Red Cross. In the following years, she joined several organizations in New York, improved her public speaking abilities, and positioned herself as a city leader.

In September 1918, while tidying up Franklin's belongings after a trip, Eleanor found love letters from his secretary, Lucy Mercer. It became clear that her husband did not love her. Eleanor wanted a divorce, but her mother-in-law opposed it to avoid a scandal that could ruin her son's political career. They finally reached an agreement: they would remain a happy couple in appearance, but her mother-in-law would, in turn, pay for a house where she and her children could live. Sara also agreed to finance her social pursuits. Despite the ugly situation,

Eleanor and Franklin remained friends and colleagues after the incident.

During a vacation trip to Canada in August 1921, he was diagnosed with polio, a paralytic illness. His wife then dedicated herself to tending to him. Nevertheless, the paralysis did not stop him from running for governor in 1928 and president in 1932, despite his mother's wishes.

This same period was when Eleanor met journalist Lorena "Hick" Hickok. She accompanied and interviewed the pair throughout the campaign trips and rallies. The two women forged a friendship that lasted years and went through different stages: from lovers, confidants, and counselors to best friends. Even among soulmates, one could argue. Their love story was kept secret for decades, but the letters they exchanged can give testimony to the affair. They expressed their physical attraction and wrote to each other with infinite love and passion. Sadly, from 1933 on, the relationship started to cool down due to Eleanor's role as the first lady. She never ceased to love her, though, as she wrote in a letter in 1938.

The role of the first lady had been, until Eleanor, merely ceremonial. She became the presidential adviser and gave countless conferences for women journalists, implemented social welfare programs, and advocated for civil women's rights. Her column in the newspaper was her medium for expressing her opinions regarding the less favored. She remains the longest-serving first lady (1933–1945). And just like Rosa Parks, she actively participated in antiracist campaigns with the National Association for the Advancement of Colored People.

When the Spanish Civil War broke out, she put her sympathies with the Republican side, and on an official visit to England, the pair adopted a Spanish boy named Kerman Mirena Iriondo from the Basque region who fled the war and was taken in by a British civil organization.

After her husband's death, she continued her political

activism. Her negotiation skills, social commitment, and experience made President Truman appoint her as a delegate of the United States to the United Nations General Assembly. He nicknamed her "the first lady of the world". Later, she became President of the United Nations Commission on Human Rights (UNCHR) and participated in drafting The Universal Declaration of Human Rights, where she requested the phrase "All men are born free..." be changed to "All human beings are born free..." a subtle but meaningful change.

Eleanor left the UN in 1951 but continued to write (publishing four books), hold conferences, and participate in the Democratic Party until her death from tuberculosis on November 7th, 1962, at the age of 78.

Emmeline Pankhurst: Deeds Before Words

Some call Emmeline Pankhurst "one of the first feminists in history." A fervent militant and political subject. She was born in the Moss Side district of Manchester, United Kingdom, on July 15, 1858, under the name Emmeline Goulden. It helped in her political upbringing that her family was quite progressive at a time when women were not allowed to vote and were treated like second-class citizens.

Her parents, Robert and Sophia Goulden, were abolitionists and in favor of equal rights for all genders. But even this could not help avoid the unequal education the family gave their ten children—their first son had died as a baby; they still wanted to make good wives and mothers out of the girls in their family.

In her autobiography, she recounts an experience that changed her forever. One night, when she was young, her father came into her room to say goodnight, but she pretended to be asleep. Unfortunately, or maybe not so, she heard him lamenting that she was not a boy. This was maybe one of the two turning points of her life.

Nevertheless, there were always books, journals, or pamphlets close by for Emmeline. One of these was the Women's Suffrage Journal, a weekly publication her mother consumed avidly. Lydia Becker, the editor of the magazine, hosted reunions often to discuss the right of women to vote. One afternoon, returning home from school, Emmeline found her mother getting ready to attend one of the meetings, to which she insisted on going. The meeting marked the beginning —the second turning point—of her life as a convinced suffragette. She was 14 years old.

At the age of 15, after successfully convincing her parents to let her study abroad, she left her hometown for Paris to attend the École Normale de Neuilly. There she studied chemistry and accounting, but also traditional subjects for women, like embroidery. Her roommate, a girl named Noémie Rochefort, became her best friend. Noémie also came from a family of political activists, which made the bond stronger. They would often share stories of their families' deeds. But after a failed attempt to marry in France, she returned to England.

Some time later, in 1878, a 20 years old Emmeline met her soon-to-be husband. His name was Richard Pankhurst, a 44 years old barrister who frequented the same social and political circles she did. He was an activist for women's suffrage and other relevant causes. Their affection was undisguisable, and even though they loved each other very much, the circumstances forced them—Emmeline would be ostracized from political life otherwise—to get married; they did so on December 18th, 1879.

The couple had six children in ten years. Sadly, the older son fell ill with diphtheria and died shortly after, at the age of four. She was left so devastated that she had a portrait painted in his honor but was never able to look at it. The younger son was born after the loss of his brother on July 7, 1889, and was the last of the children to come into the world. Emmeline had a favorite daughter—her eldest—named Christabel; she would be the one to accompany her most in politics. During this decade, she participated actively in the politics of her community, her city, and even international affairs.

The family had to relocate several times, from Emmeline's parents' cottage in Seedley to Russell Square in Bloomsbury. The home was the perfect setting for hosting political reunions of all kinds, and they did so happily. The couple founded in 1889 the Women's Franchise League (WFL), an organization advocating for women's right to vote. It supported equal rights for women in the areas of divorce and inheritance and had alliances with socialist organizations. But due to its radical approach, they encountered much resistance, and the group dissolved a year after the first meeting.

After a failed attempt at a fabric business in London for Emmeline and a poor client base for Richard, by 1893, they had decided to move back to Manchester; the family settled into a house in Manchester's Victoria Park. The following period found her collaborating with several political organizations; one of them was the Independent Labour Party (ILP), in which her activities included distributing meals to poor, unemployed people. When she was elected Poor Law Guardian in Chorlton-on-Medlock, the conditions in which people were living in that workhouse horrified and angered her. Little girls scrubbing floors, pregnant women working almost until they went into labor, and respiratory diseases were the norm.

Two years later, in 1896, she and two other men had to face legal action after they violated a court order that prohibited the ILP from holding meetings at Boggart Hole Clough. Refusing to pay the fine, the two men—Emmeline was not imprisoned, probably because she was a woman—spent a month in prison.

The episode took a toll on the Pankhurst family, both financially and physically. During the legal battle, Richard developed a gastric ulcer that accompanied him for the next two years until his body could not bear it anymore; he died on July 5, 1898.

21

Emmeline found out on her way home from London through a newspaper which another train passenger was carrying. She was never able to say her last goodbye to him.

The death of Richard forced Emmeline to look for a paying job to support her family. She was appointed as the Registrar of Births and Deaths in Chorlton and, a while later, to the Manchester School Board. And just like when she was a Poor Law Guardian, the conditions women were forced to endure made her sick and angry, both at the system for forcing these people to live under such conditions and at the people themselves for not standing up. Passivity enraged her.

By 1903, the little advancement made in women's voting had made her increasingly frustrated. Many were promises and few were actions, and given the conditions in which she saw people living, it was cruel that the individuals in decision-making positions took so much time to make significant changes. This led Emmeline, her colleagues, and her daughters to found the Women's Social and Political Union (WSPU).

The WSPU started its campaign lightly but, over time, took more and more intense measures to catch attention. One of the selected tactics was to get arrested in demonstrations to make their demands known to the public. Emmeline got arrested for the first time in 1908 and was sentenced to six weeks in prison. Tactics would become heavier in the following years, ranging from window-smashing of public buildings to hunger strikes to protest the treatment in prisons. Authorities aimed to break the hunger strikes by force-feeding the women participating, which would bring public backlash over the horrific methods used. Arson was added in 1912 when it was clear that the existing tactics were not enough.

Emmeline would spend these years traveling a lot to attend rallies and speak to the public. Sometimes she had to continue touring even if she did not want to. This was the case when her son Henry fell ill and was left paralyzed in 1909; she went on a tour of the US to earn money and pay for his treatment. But the treatment would not be enough to save him, and he passed away with his mother holding his hand on January 5, 1910.

With the outbreak of the First World War, Emmeline and Christabel decided to put the militant actions for the vote on standby. They thought their energies should be directed toward the war effort. Her other two daughters, Adela and Sylvia, had had differences with them inside the organization—authoritarian attitudes were put into question—for various reasons and left before the war was declared, and even after, the two sisters spoke against the war. Family relationships never recovered from this time.

The vote for women was finally implemented—with some restrictions—in 1918, just a few months before the end of the war. Emmeline finally achieved what she had been fighting for all those years. The win was fulfilling but, at the same time, left her devoid of a main purpose.

Nevertheless, she did not stop her political activism, going from supporting further empowerment for women to defending British imperialism and promoting "eugenic feminism" for "race betterment." These ideas seemed to be floating around at that time for anyone to catch. She even joined the Conservative Party in 1926, to the surprise of her colleagues and many more.

Emmeline's health had deteriorated because of the years of hunger strikes and imprisonment, which led her to move to a nursing home. The change would prove to be insufficient, and on June 14, 1928, she fell into a critical condition and passed away.

Her contributions remain disputed to this day and will probably remain that way in the future. What is undeniable is her brutal drive to bring about change.

As discussed before, our values are given to us or chosen by us according to our environment. Starting with the example of Rosa Parks: She was not born with the set of values she later developed. Her surroundings transformed her into an activist; that is to say, racism made her an anti-racist, and having seen with her own eyes the terrible violence inflicted on people like her and the long-lasting impact of that violence made her choose non-violent ways.

We can clearly distinguish the two conflicting sets of values in society—cultural and personal. One set supported segregation—that is what was right and desirable—while the other set pushed for inclusion—mixing and equality were the right and desirable outcomes. These conflicts brought many problems and sufferings for Rosa and her family; she had to move and lost her job; she spent years receiving death threats; she was pushed aside by the same people who were supposed to help and support her. Despite all of this, she never gave up on her personal values until the societal norms—the cultural values' transformation would take longer if it were not still taking place to this day—transformed into what she thought was right and fair. She could have succumbed to fear, but she never did and continued on her quest for a change. Her values defined her purpose and were her anchors of inner strength.

Eleanor can be said to hold similar values to Rosa. They advocated for an antiracist, equal society. What is different about them is their surroundings. This only proves that cultural values are important but not determinant; she could have kept doing politics aimed at maintaining her privilege, but she did not. Eleanor's privilege played another big role in the impact of her values on the world; while Rosa was threatened and encountered violent resistance, Eleanor's was not so resisted. This example might give reason to have many different people push for cultural changes at every moment, even if they are not experiencing the suffering themselves. We do not have the luxury of excluding the power of empathy for change.

Emmeline, on the other hand, is the example of the chapter on what it means to change some values throughout a lifetime. She started her political life with ties to some socialist organizations and finished it with ties to the conservative party and advocating for "race betterment" when she had seen the lives and heard the stories of the women at "the bottom" of her society. If, at first, she was advocating for the well-being of these women in need, at the end of her life, she let her personal values be *contaminated* by the ideas or values of other people—ideas that would later become cultural values and societal norms in some countries. She had always been aware of the conflicting relationship between her personal values and the cultural values of her time, and she embraced wholeheartedly her own values until the norms finally changed. So, the question of what made her change so radically will remain.

Her daughters, Adela and Sylvia, left her side because of her authoritarian ways inside the WSPU, and could never repair their relationship. The letters they exchanged bear testimony to how she saw her daughters as disappointments. And in clear contrast to Rosa, it is worth wondering how much more Emmeline would have achieved for the rights of women if she had chosen a more peaceful way of resisting.

Values describe the personal qualities we choose or the kind of person we want to become, the manner in which we respect and treat others and ourselves, and how we interact with our environment and the world around us; they are like a lighthouse in dark and stormy waters, steering us in the right direction. Our values define the kind of action we will take, especially in challenging circumstances when we experience setbacks and failures. Choosing our values means choosing our behaviors. Certainly, Emmeline is an example of it.

An Invitation for Reflection to Define Your Values and a Call to Action to Grow Resilience

- Write down 20 or more values that you believe are important. Pick the three or four that you deem are the most important to you, reflect upon them, take notes of your thoughts, and then write a short essay about those values, answering some of the following questions:
- What exactly is the meaning of those values, and what do these values mean to you?
- Why are they important to you?
- When was the last time you noticed that you actively made a decision based on your values? In what kind of situation did that happen, and how was that helpful to you?

Keep those values written on a card in your wallet or on your phone, so you can easily refer back to them when it gets tough.

3

CHOOSING OUR PASSIONS

Passion is Energy: Feel the power that comes from focusing on what excites you. –Oprah Winfrey

INTRODUCTION

P assion: A word everybody encounters often—it can be used as a compliment—*you do things with true passion*—or a judgment—*you are too passionate!* The main difference between these two, however, is whether they are attached to reason or not. One is desirable, while the other might be dangerous.

The opposite feeling, apathy, is certainly not desirable at all. As common knowledge puts it: Passion is what gives purpose and meaning to our finite lives. Where to put that passion is entirely up to you.

What It Means to Be Passionate

According to Merriam-Webster (2019), passion or passions:

- "The emotions as distinguished from reason."
- "Intense, driving, or overmastering feelings or conviction."
- "Ardent affection: Love."
- "A strong liking or desire for or devotion to some activity, object, or concept."
- "An object of desire or deep interest."

Note that one of these definitions involves love and desire, and the other lacks reason.

The APA Dictionary (n.d.) defines passion:

- "An intense, driving, or overwhelming feeling or conviction. Passion is often contrasted with emotion in that passion affects a person unwillingly."
- "A strong enthusiasm for or devotion to an activity, object, concept, or the like."

The word originates from the ancient Greek word *pathein*, which means "to suffer; to be acted on," the late Latin *passio*, a Christian term meaning "passion; suffering," and the Latin word, *pati* meaning "to suffer."

The word origin tells us something slightly different; we can infer from it a definition closer to a "willingness to suffer for what we love." Subtle but meaningful.

In the neuroscience realm, researchers have long stated that doing what we love has a positive impact on the brain and body, making us happier and stronger. One aspect of this is the desire to expand our performances—physical or mental—beyond our current limits.

There are two stages to the process of improving: Exploring and connecting. The first stage is about personal work towards the goal of improving, and the second stage involves connection and sharing the passion with other people. Even passions are collective. A feedback loop is inevitable.

In terms of the biochemistry of the brain, dopamine, oxytocin, and norepinephrine are the neurotransmitters and hormones involved. Dopamine favors exploration by giving us a sense of pleasure when released into the brain. It is not the reward feeling but rather the anticipation of reward. Oxytocin, on the other hand, has a soothing effect when released in the brain during social interaction; it increases empathy, generosity, and trust. Once these stages are followed sufficiently often, the brain adapts to the habits by molding new patterns, making it easier for us to obtain better results from our passion.

With all this knowledge, let us now dive into the lives of passionate women.

WOMEN WHO FOLLOWED THEIR PASSIONS

Nora Ephron: The Art of Not Taking Oneself Too Seriously

When Harry Met Sally or *You've Got Mail*, is there someone who has not watched or heard about those movies? Nora Louise Ephron was the mastermind behind both films. She was born on May 19, 1941, in New York City to Henry Ephron and Pheobe Wolkind. She was the eldest of four girls in a Jewish family.

When Nora was five years old, the family moved to Beverly Hills, a change she was not pleased with. In one of her interviews, she recalled the experience as being "ripped out" of a place she thought she belonged to. The couple had decided to move there to become screenwriters for Hollywood. It would turn out to be a family of writers, as Nora's sisters Delia, Hallie, and Amy would all grow up to become writers themselves. Something in the genes, no doubt.

Her parents would later become alcoholics, with her mother dying of cirrhosis, and even though Nora experienced these tragic events in her life, she was never grim. Perhaps because it was her younger sister who took on the worst part.

She always knew she wanted to be a journalist; Lois Lane— an award-winning journalist and Superman's love interest—was probably to blame for that, but it was during her high school years that she found the inspiration to become a journalist. Charles Simms, the journalism teacher at Beverly Hills High School, appointed her to run the newspaper and encouraged her to pursue the path. She graduated in 1958 and continued her education at Wellesley College—a liberal arts private college for women—in Massachusetts, where she graduated in 1962 with a degree in political science.

She worked as an intern at the White House for a short period of time. At the same time, she applied for a position as a writer at Newsweek. She got a job, just not the one she was hoping for; the newspaper did not hire women writers, so she took on a mail-girl position. But it was not enough for someone like her, so she quit soon after. She went on to work for a satirical magazine, where she shook things up a little bit. During a newspaper strike in New York, she had the idea to make a parody of the New York Post and its leading columnist, Leonard Lyons; they named it the New York Pest. There were two possible outcomes to this: getting sued or getting hired. That is how she got a job trial at the paper.

She was hired as a reporter and covered everything she could, from murders to politics, trials, social life, and even movie stars. Despite the seriousness of some topics, she always said it was a lot of fun; it suited her dark sense of humor. She worked there for five years. In those years, Nora met writer Dan Greenburg, her first husband, whom she married in 1967 after a year of dating.

At the time, there were not many women writing for New York magazines, but if they were good enough, they could enter the select group. And Nora did. She was writing pieces for

Cosmopolitan, The New York Times Sunday Magazine, and New York. By 1970, she had the opportunity to start writing a column for Esquire. In her lines, she would make fun of everyone, including herself. Journalism may have been her job, but humor was her art.

In the next decade, she steadily grew a fanbase with her witty columns, and while her professional life was flourishing—with her columns gathered as a book—her personal life was not so much. Six years after the wedding, Nora and Dan got divorced; they never had children. Some time later, she met Carl Bernstein, also a journalist; they got married in 1976. Nobody could accuse her of lacking faith in romance.

Carl Bernstein and Bob Woodward's book about the Watergate scandal, *All the President's Men*, had the first script written by William Goldman, but neither of them was satisfied with the result. Nora and Carl ended up rewriting the script, something that taught her a lot about the craft. This was her first attempt at screenwriting. And even though their script was never used, someone in Hollywood read it and offered Nora her first screenwriting gig; the script was for a television movie. It ended up being "one of the worst things I've ever seen" (KCTS 9, 2011), in her words.

Nora's bet on romance paid off in a way that would have broken others, but for her, it was the source of inspiration. In 1979, she had a two-year-old son, Jacob, and was pregnant with her second child, Max, when she found out her husband was having an affair with Margaret Jay, a British journalist, and herself married.

Her mother would always say a phrase to Nora and her sisters, "Everything is copy." She taught her girls to laugh. Especially at the hardest moments of life, do not let anyone else laugh first; make a good story about it and move on. So she did. She sat down for two years—with breaks in between to do screenplays and get paid—to write a book about her divorce with some elements of fiction in it. She named it—very appropriately—*Heartburn*, which was published in 1983. The screenplays did not get made into movies until *Silkwood*, in that same year. It was a script she worked on with her friend Alice Arlen; it was directed by Mike Nichols, and starring in it was none other than Meryl Streep. Alice and Nora were nominated for Best Original Screenplay at the 1984 Oscars.

The book had immense success, and the movie—which Nora adapted into a screenplay herself—came out in 1986. Mike Nichols directed again, Meryl Streep acted again, and Jack Nicholson played the hateful husband. The real hateful ex-husband threatened to sue but never went through with it. The pages did not fall short of mockery.

That year, she started working on one of the most influential romantic comedies of all time: *When Harry Met Sally*. The film starring Meg Ryan and Billy Crystal premiered in 1989, and its most iconic scene—with Meg Ryan's character faking an orgasm—was a collaborative work between actors, writers, and the director Rob Reiner. An Oscar nomination came about again for Nora.

In the meantime, she had time for yet another bet on romance; Nora married screenwriter Nicholas Pileggi in 1987.

As she had been doing since her graduation, every eight to ten years, she took on new professional challenges. And so the natural course of things was for Nora to progress into something other than writing scripts. In 1992, she became a director with the film *This Is My Life*. Her sister Delia wrote the script alongside her, based on a book called *This is Your Life* by Meg Wolitzer. She continued to direct and write over the next few years until another big hit came along: *You've Got Mail*. Meg Ryan and Tom Hanks played the star couple. The hit was released in 1998.

The turn of the century found Nora writing and producing. In 2002, she wrote her first Broadway play, *Imaginary Friends*.

Later, she worked with her sister again to write another play called *Love, Loss, and What I Wore*. In 2006, almost 24 years after her last book, she published *I Feel Bad About My Neck: And Other Thoughts on Being a Woman*, an acid take on getting old.

At that time, she was diagnosed with myelodysplasia but decided not to let anyone outside her close family know. Nevertheless, she continued to write a blog for The Huffington Post and write and direct another movie: *Julie & Julia*, with Meryl Streep and Amy Adams.

She died on June 26, 2012, due to complications from pneumonia. Her complicated and interesting female characters remain part of her legacy and give testimony to the fact that complex characters can draw a large audience.

Clara Schumann: A Passionate Life of Music

Clara Josephine Schumann was born Clara Josephine Wieck in Leipzig, Kingdom of Saxony, German Confederation. She came into the world on September 13th, 1819, at a time when the current state of Germany did not exist. It was a short period after the dissolution of the Holy Roman Empire in 1806 when the Napoleonic Wars started to take place. The German Confederation had been formed four years prior to Clara's birth.

Her parents, Friedrich Wieck and Marianne Tromlitz, were both pianists and piano teachers. Friedrich owned a music shop as well. They had five children over the course of eight years. Tragically, their first child died a year after his birth. Clara was their second child and the oldest of three more sons: Alwin, Gustav, and Viktor.

At the age of four, Clara began to take piano lessons at home from her mother. Marianne, less than happy with her husband's controlling ways, left him for her then-lover Adolph Bargiel, a friend of the family. Friedrich got custody of the four children but agreed to let Clara live with her mother until her fifth birthday. Mother and daughter would continue in regular contact until Marianne and Adolph got married and moved to Berlin.

After the divorce, a housekeeper took care of the children. Once Clara returned to her father's home, he planned a schedule for her: Almost every learning hour of the day would be spent studying music, from piano and violin to composition. It would not be an exaggeration to call Friedrich a control freak, so much so that she did not have any friends her age growing up.

Immersed in that world, Clara began accompanying her father to concerts when she was very young. This allowed her to be known, and lo and behold, she made her debut at the age of nine at the Gewandhaus concert hall in Leipzig on October 28, 1828. The same year, Friedrich married Clementine Fechner, a girl who was twenty years his junior.

During Clara's tours, she would meet another pianist by the name of Robert Schumann. The boy was 19 at the time and studied law, which he dropped to attend music lessons with Friedrich. He rented a room in the Wiecks' home and stayed for a year.

By that time, people were already calling her a child prodigy. Over the next couple of years, Clara went touring around Europe with her father acting as her manager. It was undeniable that Friedrich lived through his daughter's success and, to some extent, live from her earnings. At the age of 14, she played her own *Piano Concerto* for the first time.

Robert Schumann and Clara continued their friendship, and when she turned 16, Friedrich found out they were in love. He disapproved of the relationship and sent the girl away to Dresden. Nevertheless, they secretly continued to write to each other. A year later, Robert formally asked Friedrich for her daughter's hand, which he refused. To try and separate them, he sent his daughter on constant tours around Europe. Between December 1837 and April 1838, Clara gave a series of recitals in

Vienna that made her gain the utmost recognition, both from the public and her colleagues, a group that included Chopin and Liszt.

The following year, Clara's desire was to perform in Paris, but her father refused to go or let her governess accompany her. Nonetheless, a French woman was hired to chaperone her, and Clara herself managed the entire tour, making use of the skills her father had taught her.

Seeing that Friedrich would not consent to Clara and Robert's marriage, the couple decided to appeal to the Dresden court for their right to marry. In June, Clara filed a lawsuit, which made her father throw her out of the house. Fortunately, Marianne took her in, and Robert helped her financially while she settled in. Once done, she went on to perform in Hamburg and Bremen, earning some money.

In December 1839, Friedrich presented his own declaration to the court, slandering Robert and Clara. This was a humiliation for both of them, adding one more to the collection of actions he had taken in his quest to stop the marriage. A few months later, Robert sued him back for it, but in June 1840, the court finally ruled in favor of the couple. They got married the day before Clara turned 21—and attained majority status—on the 12th of September 1840. She had a defiant fire in her. Despite Friedrich's slander, Clara gave several concerts around the country with much praise, reaffirming her independence and confidence. Two years later, Friedrich finally came to his senses and reconciled with his daughter. He was yearning to see his grandchildren.

During their marriage, they composed several pieces together, and Clara arranged some of her husband's instrumental compositions for the piano. She would also play some of these pieces for the public. In addition to her duties as a mother, she also took care of household management and financial affairs. Though rare for a woman then, she continued to earn an income by giving concerts and piano lessons. And it was a fortunate decision, as she would become the sole breadwinner of the family not long after the marriage.

The couple had eight children—four girls and four boys—and Clara was pregnant 10 times over fourteen years. Their first son, Emil, born in 1846, died only a year after his birth. Her first three daughters—Marie, Elise, and Julie—were born in 1841, 1843, and 1845, respectively.

In 1844, Robert suffered a big manic episode—a symptom of bipolar disorder—and the doctors recommended they move to Dresden. The same year, Clara met Joseph Joachim, a 14-year-old violinist who would later become a friend and play innumerable concerts with her throughout their lives. Two years later, fortunately, Robert was feeling better. Their four younger children—Ludwig, Ferdinand, Eugenie, and Felix—were born in 1848, 1849, 1851, and 1854.

The family traveled continuously due to the couple's tours and also attended concerts. In one May-of-1853 concert, although it was not the first time they had heard Joseph Joachim play, his performance of Beethoven's *Violin Concerto* left them ecstatic. During those months, Joseph met Johannes Brahms, a young composer. The two very soon developed a fondness for each other that would make Joseph set it as his goal to introduce the young man to the Schumanns. With this intention, he wrote a letter of presentation to the couple and sent Brahms away to knock on their door in Dusseldorf.

Friendships were always important in the Schumanns' lives. That is why, when Robert had a mental collapse and attempted suicide by jumping into the Rhine—he was saved by fishermen—in 1854, friends were always there to support Clara and her children. For two years, he was admitted to a sanatorium in Endenich, and Brahms visited him often. Contrary to Brahms, Clara was not allowed to visit him until two days before his death on July 29, 1856. His suffering broke her heart, but she was relieved when fate liberated him from his pain.

In April 1856, Clara performed her first concert in England with Joseph and Italian cellist Alfredo Piatti. She would come back to tour every year for the next 15. After Robert's death, she continued to tour Germany and many other countries but composed only one more piece and dedicated herself mostly to editing her late husband's compositions. If, at first, she had believed she could be a talented composer, later life brought her doubts and pessimism. Her context led her to think she could not do it, as she was a woman and probably the only one in her pursuits.

Brahms was Clara's closest friend, and to this day, academics still argue whether they were a couple. In his letters throughout the years, he showed immense love and respect for her. So much so that after Robert's death, he declared his love for her. Some of these letters would later be burned by Clara herself, with her daughter Marie trying and succeeding in convincing her not to do so. Guilt was perhaps the fuel for this action.

Her daughter Julie would die in 1872, leaving two children for Clara to take care of. In 1878, she was offered a position as the principal piano teacher at the Hoch Conservatory in Frankfurt. The next year, her son Felix died, leaving his two children for Clara to raise. In 1891, her son Ferdinand died at the age of 42. Ludwig had probably inherited his father's mental disorder and was institutionalized like him. She had to witness so many of her children die before her, something that probably would have broken other people but not her.

Tragedies were commonplace in Clara's life, but that did not stop her from following the path—with its unexpected turns— she had designed for herself. But not only did she do it for herself but also for her grandchildren, who depended on her.

Old age brought her difficulties walking, and she needed a wheelchair to move around. She became partially deaf as well.

She gave her last concert in 1891 but continued teaching until her death at age 76 from a stroke on May 20, 1896. Brahms was inconsolable over the loss of the love of his life and followed her a year later. Her remains were buried alongside her husband's in Bonn.

Even though her husband's name has outshone hers, her talent needs to be acknowledged and celebrated. What else could she have created if she had not been discouraged by circumstances from unleashing her creativity?

Coco Chanel: Design as a Lifestyle

There is no need to explain the weight Coco Chanel has in history, especially in the history of fashion. The last name itself carries the weight of an industry. Nevertheless, I will try to recount her extraordinary life.

Gabrielle Bonheur Chanel was the name her parents gave her. Perhaps to encourage her or bless her in some way, they named her *Bonheur*—literally, happiness or good luck in French. Not without a hint of irony, the last name we came to know so well associated with glamour and luxury was misspelled—and never corrected—as "Chasnel" on Gabrielle's birth certificate.

She was born on August 19, 1883, in Saumur, Maine-et-Loire, west of France, to a poor family as the second child. Her parents, Eugénie Jeanne Devolle Chanel and Albert Chanel were both hard-working people; Jeanne was a laundrywoman, and Albert was an itinerant street clothes vendor. Her older sister's name was Julia; only a year set the two apart. After them, four more children would come into the family: Alphonse, born in 1885; Antoinette, born in 1887; Lucien; and Augustin, who sadly died at six months old.

The family had a very unstable financial situation and lived like nomads, moving around from one questionable lodging to the next quite often; none of the children attended school. Sadly, her mother, Jeanne, died young, at the age of 32, when Gabrielle was only 11. Somewhat lost after her death, Albert decided to send the boys to work on different farms and the girls to the convent of Aubazine. There, the girls would learn how to sew and embroider. Turning 18, Gabrielle could no longer stay at the orphanage and, therefore, left for a boarding house for Catholic girls in Moulins.

During those years, she worked as a seamstress in the daytime and as a singer at night. In Café-concerts, special establishments military officers loved to visit for entertainment, she would make her pocket money singing in between shows of the more renowned performers. Here is where she acquired the nickname, Coco, from singing *Qui qu'a vu Coco dans l'Trocadéro?*; the audience would call for her with the nickname. After a failed attempt at a singing career, as she was not particularly gifted—much to her dismay—she decided to pursue other paths.

Éttiene Balsan was her first partner, whom she met while working as a singer. He was a textile heir and the one who introduced her to this world. As a cavalry officer, he would depart for military campaigns, often leaving her alone in his Château Royallieu near Compiègne. Out of boredom, Coco began designing hats as a pastime.

In 1908, she met Arthur Edward Capel, a very wealthy friend of Éttiene and a polo player, and began an affair with him as well. Later in life, she would admit that Arthur was the love of her life. The following year, she moved to Paris and installed herself in an apartment Arthur had lent her.

Coco's career as a milliner began in 1910, when she got a license and opened a shop in Paris. At first, she designed only hats, but with her success, she expanded into deluxe leisurewear. With the financial support of Arthur, she opened two more boutiques in Deauville and Biarritz in 1913 and 1915, respectively. Her work introduced new designs with well-known fabrics. Within a year, she was able to return the investment Arthur had supported her with.

Her originality consisted of using textiles that would not normally be used for women's clothing. This made the pieces comfortable for everyday life, something women were eager to wear after the war. She is credited with changing the female silhouette by getting rid of the corset and countless layers of fabric and adopting a more relaxed and masculine style. Probably one of the most important pieces of clothing today, the little black cocktail dress, was imposed by the brand.

In 1919, Coco registered as a *couturière*—a dressmaker—and established her brand as Maison Chanel. But tragedy would hit her by the end of that year; Arthur died in a car accident. Although they had ended the relationship two years before, and he had married another woman, they never quite cut off contact. Her world fell apart with his departure, but she continued to work regardless.

Over the next years, she would meet Composer Igor Stravinsky, Duke Hugh Richard Arthur Grosvenor of Westminster, and Edward VIII, Prince of Wales, all of whom would become her lovers, some confirmed and others mere rumors. All of these men would serve as inspiration for her designs, from Arthur's whisky bottle for her perfume to the tailored tweed suits the Duke wore.

After Arthur's death, Coco was in need of a new business partner, as women could not—and would not until 1965—have bank accounts to their names. Among the many wealthy men she knew, Pierre Wertheimer had experience with luxury fashion brands. In 1924, he and his brother became her partners and investors. They signed a contract that would allow her to continue with her business and grow even larger while giving up 90 percent of the profits from the sales of the brand's signature scent, Chanel No. 5. She had, for all intents and purposes, lent her name to the Wertheimers' perfume company to independently produce, distribute, and market her creation. It was around this time that the famous logo of the two interlocked C's was unveiled.

The 1930s brought more success to the brand but also political turmoil: The rise of Nazi Germany and the coming of the Second World War. She had already designed the dance costumes for the *Ballets Russes*, but the new decade saw her go into film costume art. She dressed several Hollywood stars but came to despise the place. Even though her Hollywood experience was not what she had expected, she continued to design for French cinema. In 1933, Coco's affair with the Duke of Westminster came to an end after ten long years. Just like with men, Coco had a close relationship with drugs; she started injecting morphine around this time and would never cease until the end of her days.

When the German troops invaded the capital in 1940, she was forced to close all her stores except for one, laying off thousands of workers. She then moved into the Hotel Ritz, where the Germans set up their center of operations. Baron Hans Gunther von Dincklage, a senior German officer and attorney, became her lover during the occupation. This part of Coco's life remains heavily questioned to this day. She was accused of being a Nazi collaborator and spy, with some people claiming she was antisemitic herself and not only an opportunist. The speculation comes from her days as the Duke's lover, a declared antisemite and homophobic. Under the occupation's imposed anti-Jewish business laws, she tried to take back control of her perfume branch. The Wertheimers were Jewish and had to give up their company to a Christian friend and flee the country. They got it back after the war, and this fact would prove important for Coco later.

Once the occupation of France ended in 1944 and Coco could leave the country, she was arrested and interrogated. Though thousands of citizens went to trial for treason, she was not charged due to "lack of evidence," despite German officers testifying she did spy for them during the said occupation. Theories regarding the reasons pointed in the direction of Winston Churchill—he had known and befriended her for many years—and other elite British citizens wanting to keep the secrets she knew hidden. Others suggest she used her influence and paid people off to come out free of charge.

Quite naturally, *La Maison Chanel* came crashing down along with her reputation, so she fled to Switzerland, where she stayed for almost a decade. But the urge to design and be relevant in the fashion world again brought her back to Paris. In 1954, at age 74 and with the help of Pierre Wertheimer—the same man she had sued in 1947 to renegotiate the 1924 contract—Coco reopened her fashion house. Her collections were poorly received in France but loved by Hollywood and American celebrities. Eventually, she was able to return to the fashion summit.

Still living at the Ritz, Coco worked until the last days of her life. She had a few friends and confidants but had become lonelier throughout the years. Death was found in her sleep on January 10, 1971, at the age of 87. Many illustrious names attended her funeral at the Église de la Madeleine, and she was buried in the Bois-de-Vaux Cemetery, Lausanne, in Switzerland.

HOW TO FOLLOW YOUR PASSION AND BUILD RESILIENCE

The stories of Nora, Clara, and Coco all share the element of passion for film and writing, music, and design.

Nora had an innate passion and an upbringing that helped her develop her craft. From her mother demanding that she and her sisters tell their days in interesting ways when arriving home from school to her teachers, they all saw a genuine interest in her from a young age and watered that drive to grow into what it became later.

She found a scathing style and humorous voice of her own that many people liked, and many others feared. The bad moments in her life were used as fuel for her passion for story-telling, giving birth to iconic pieces of pop culture. Something about what she believed she needed to say, the world needed to hear.

Clara's passion, music, was also nurtured by her parents and surroundings. But for her, it was very different; she was never given the option not to do music. It is fortunate that she actually loved music and continued to love it all her life.

And just like Nora, we can clearly see the stages of exploring and connecting within their respective fields. Clara shared music with her husband, friends, and family, while Nora worked with friends, her sister, and her husband. When connecting with other people with shared passions, their perspectives and constructive opinions can complement and boost our passions.

In the case of Coco, her path seemed to be a lonely one. Her family had little to do with her love for fashion; she found it along the way. Her passion was strong, and even when she was in another country, and her name had almost faded away, it would not let her sit by. She moved back to Paris and began again. We can even tie a word already seen in this text to Coco: conviction. Faith and passion connect with each other as both are strong convictions.

Her independent mind was convinced of her vision for what fashion needed to become for women—not just beautiful but functional as well. She was dedicated to her passion with immense creativity and a fresh take, leading the industry to places it had not been before.

When we are passionate about something, our entire body gets aligned with this passion. All of a sudden, we are able to mobilize energies we did not know we had; we are focused, and despite working for hours, we still feel energized. Time seems to fly by, and other things become less important in our daily lives. It can even be compared to falling in love with someone.

We can use this to our advantage by redirecting that passion toward positive things rather than spending our energies on negative experiences. Every time we talk about the difficult events in our lives, we put ourselves in the same vibration and emotions we experienced then; it becomes a vicious circle, taking away our energy, our focus, and the possibility of developing our superpowers again and again. The opposite happens when we talk about something we are passionate about; we *lighten up* inside and become receptive to new ideas, possibilities, and solutions. That passion becomes our drive—the reason to get out of bed every day. This is the first step to unlocking the part of our brain that holds the "energy of our inner genius."

Clara Schuman was an example of redirected passion who taught us how important it is to enjoy life's beauty; "Why hurry over beautiful things? Why not linger and enjoy them?" (n.d.). This was her motto, in spite of all the hardships and losses she experienced. This is probably why she *lived* music all her life.

Passions create a sense of meaning and purpose, and in turn, this provides us with feelings of inner valuation and self-valuation. With this passion within us, we are less reliant on external validation and are willing to follow our path even without support, approval, or acknowledgment from others. In a world of social media *likes and comments*, we sometimes seem to forget this. Our passions help us find our validation and make us more independent from outside critics, a process that allows us to grow resilience.

Questions and Exercises to Define Your Passion and Grow Resilience

- In a journal, write down what you are passionate about and why you are passionate about it.
- When you look back to a younger version of yourself, what was your passion then? Has it changed over time? Or have you just lost track of your passion, and now is the time to "get back to it"?
- For one day, pay attention to how much time you spend thinking about your problems and difficulties and how much time you spend thinking about your passion. Keep a record in the journal and write down how it makes you feel. Do you notice a difference in your body between problem-thinking and passion-thinking? Over time, there will be a moment when you will spend more time thinking and acting in your area of passion, and your life will begin to change.

4

MAPPING OUR VISION AND DIRECTION

Without vision, you have no direction. Without direction, you have no purpose. –Steve Gilliland

INTRODUCTION

Have you ever been in a situation where you felt you faced a challenge greater than you could overcome? Where you are only feeling helpless, desperate, out of control, maybe uncoordinated at best, or in extreme situations, even chaotic? You surely have; otherwise, you would not be reading this book.

Remember that moment and the emotions. Resentment, anger, self-pity, doubt, and a lack of self-confidence may come to mind. And while all these are valid and easy to understand, they have their place but do not serve us in the long run.

Having these intense and unpleasant emotions is often a response to our circumstances—circumstances we do not expect and do not want to experience, that are painful, or that cause enormous stress. When we feel overwhelmed in such situations, it is easy to lose direction, and giving up feels tempting to alleviate the pain. In those moments, we need a clear vision to hold onto, as it gives us the guidance and stamina to continue on our path.

This strategy will guide you in building resilience by having a vision, identifying your purpose, and navigating through challenging circumstances while staying on the path of your chosen direction. Holding a clear vision of your passion and building it on belief and faith will get you through the obstacles in front of you.

The three women whose stories you are about to read found direction and had a vision for their futures. They faced countless setbacks, and some lost their lives while achieving their dreams. None of us know how much time we are given on this earth so we ought to follow our vision and dreams.

Defining Vision and Direction

Before going further, we need to set up a few definitions. The word vision has many meanings, and that is also a strength; you can choose which one to focus on. According to the dictionary, some relevant meanings for vision are (Merriam-Webster, 2019):

- "The act or power of seeing: Sight."

- a. "Something seen in a dream, trance, or ecstasy."
  b. "A thought, concept, or object formed by the imagination."
  c. "A manifestation to the senses of something immaterial."

- a. "The act or power of imagination."
  b. (1) "Mode of seeing or conceiving."
     (2) "Unusual discernment or foresight."

c. "Direct mystical awareness of the supernatural, usually in visible form."

- a. "Something seen."
  b. "A lovely or charming sight."

The APA Dictionary (n.d.) gives us the following definition of vision:

- "The sense of sight, in which the eye is the receptor,   and the stimulus is radiant energy in the visible   spectrum."
- "A visual hallucination often involving a religious or mystical experience."
- "A mental image of something or someone produced by the imagination."

Now for direction (Merriam-Webster, n.d.):

- "Guidance or supervision of action or conduct: Management."
- a. "An explicit instruction: Order."
  b. "Assistance in pointing out the proper route."
- "The line or course on which something is moving or is aiming to move, or along which something is pointing or facing."
- a. "A channel or direct course of thought or action."
  b. "A guiding, governing, or motivating purpose."
- "The art and technique of supervising the production of a show or performance: the art and technique of directing an orchestra, band, or a show (as for stage or screen)."

The last definition holds a special meaning if you think about your life as a show, with the best possible connotation—you and only you are directing.

In these definitions, we can distinguish three categories of vision, in addition to the literal meaning of vision as eyesight:

- **Intellectual vision:** This is the supernatural knowledge of a revealed truth presented to our minds. We could call it intuition as well. These can present themselves as already-acquired ideas or divine symbols, which allows the person to understand the revelation better.
- **Imaginary:** The reactions the imagination—the brain —has when reality is perceived through the senses but without the actual perception of reality. It is only a reaction to an external event.
- **Corporeal:** "A supernatural manifestation of an object to the eyes of the body." There are two versions of this vision. One can be "a figure really present that strikes the retina, and there determines the physical phenomenon of the vision, or an agent superior to man directly modifies the visual organ and produces in the composite a sensation equivalent to that which an external object would produce" (New Advent, 2021).

THREE WOMEN WHO HAD VISION AND DIRECTION

Amelia Earhart: The Wings of Icarus

Amelia Mary Earhart was born on July 24, 1897, in Atchinson, a small town in the state of Kansas. Her parents, Samuel Stanton Earhart, a lawyer, and Amelia Otis, a wealthy heir, had her and another girl, Grace Muriel, born two years after Amelia. The pair went by the nicknames Meeley and Pidge, which they would keep well into adulthood.

It was in her mother's family home that Amelia and her sister grew up in great comfort. As children, the two sisters were restless and often engaged in games "unsuitable for girls." Their father Samuel, worked as a claim officer for the Rock Island Railroad, and in 1907, he was transferred to Des Moines, Iowa.

During the transition period from Atchinson to Des Moines, the girls remained in their grandparent's home and were home-schooled. Amelia was an avid reader and would spend hours in her home's library. Once the move was over, they were enrolled in a local public school.

Curiously, the first encounter Amelia had with flying man-made devices was at age ten, when she attended the Iowa State Fair. There, Samuel encouraged her to get on a plane, but she did not care for it and refused. Little did this girl know.

Although the family seemed to have a stable financial situation, Samuel was an alcoholic, and after some time, he would be forced to retire. He rehabilitated but never got his job back. The family's circumstances deteriorated with Amelia's grandmother's sudden death, forcing them to move from place to place. She would finish high school in Chicago and enter Ogontz School in Rydal, Pennsylvania, only to drop out to volunteer for the war efforts in Toronto.

Amelia, along with her sister, enlisted as nurse's aides in 1917 and remained so until the end of World War I. The tasks included tending to wounded pilots, a circumstance that allowed Amelia to immerse herself in the world of aviation through the stories these men shared. The following year, the Spanish flu pandemic struck, and Amelia fell ill. Bored as she must have been while recovering, she studied mechanics and learned how to play the banjo. Unfortunately, she suffered from chronic sinusitis as an aftereffect for the rest of her life.

Not long after, she attended a flying exhibition in Ontario, Canada. A show was to take place; a skilled pilot would make a demonstration for the attendees. The fighter ace, playing funny, flew very close to where Amelia and a friend were standing, trying to scare the women away. Not only did he not succeed in scaring Amelia away, but the action was taken as a challenge and aroused a sense of defiance, forcing her to stand her ground. It was an adrenaline kick.

After a few attempts to enroll in universities—Smith College in Massachusetts and Columbia in New York—she reunited with her parents in California. In the last days of 1920, Amelia and her father attended an aerial meet, where she booked a flight of ten minutes in a biplane. The experience left a life-changing impression on her and was the final push she needed to make the decision to become a pilot.

To do so, she borrowed money from her mother and saved to reach the $1,000 goal, which was the cost of flying lessons. Her first instructor was a famous aviator by the name of Neta Snook. The style of the time was for women pilots to cut their hair short and wear leather jackets, so she did exactly that.

For the first six months of training, Amelia used a Curtiss JN-4 biplane until the moment she could purchase her first aircraft, a secondhand yellow Kinner Airster biplane, which she nicknamed "The Canary." Although she had a bumpy beginning, in 1922, she set a world altitude record for a woman flying at 14000 feet. A year later, Amelia got her international license as a pilot and became the 16th woman in the U.S. to reach the milestone.

Due to the financial crisis of the 20s, she was later forced to sell The Canary and take up a job as a teacher and social worker. Taking care of people was always in her blood. By 1927, she had joined the American Aeronautical Society and started writing columns promoting women in aviation for local newspapers and books about her adventures in the skies.

One day, she got a phone call from Captain. Hilton Railey. She had been chosen to be the first woman to fly across the Atlantic Ocean, and he wanted to know if she was willing. Her answer was, naturally, yes. They flew a Fokker F.VIIb/3m, and it took them 20 hours and 40 minutes to complete the flight, departing from Trepassey Harbor, Newfoundland, and arriving at Pwll near Burry Port, South Wales.

After the feat was completed, she was interviewed and admitted to having been little more than a passenger but was eager to try it alone some other time. Back in her own country, rivers of ink were flowing, telling the story of the "Queen of the Air." Cosmopolitan offered her the position of associate editor, and companies were quarreling to have her as their brands' face.

In 1929, she participated in her first air race at the Women's Air Derby—a several-day race from Santa Monica to Cleveland— or the "Powder Puff Derby," as some called it. Thanks to the race, she met other women pilots and founded The Ninety-Nines, an organization for the promotion of women in aviation. The organization, with Amelia as its president, fought for women's rights to fly and participate in races. Around the same time, she could finally acquire a new plane, a Lockheed Vega 5B.

Little has been said about her love life; after breaking up a previous engagement with Chemical Engineer Samuel Chapman a few years before, Amelia married her publisher George Putnam—at last—in 1931. The man, who was a divorcee, had asked her to marry him six times with no success. Their marriage would be one with rules set by them and nobody else: Respect and equality. As proof of this, Amelia kept her surname. On occasion, she needed her space alone, as she felt the life of a married woman was not enough. The couple never had children, but George had two sons from his previous marriage. Happily, both liked Amelia very much.

With the idea still in her mind of crossing the ocean alone and thus becoming the first woman to do so, she planned ahead.

On May 20, 1932, she took off from Newfoundland, on the east coast of Canada. She carried a thermos bottle with soup and a can of tomato juice and kept herself awake by smelling salt. Nearly 15 hours later, she landed on a pasture north of Derry in Northern Ireland, where two farmers confirmed and witnessed her deed.

Amelia became famous worldwide, not only as the first woman to achieve the flight but also as the first person to do it twice and in the shortest period of time. She was decorated multiple times by President Hoover and Congress. As women engaged in activism in their respective fields, it was only a matter of time before Eleanor Roosevelt and Amelia met and became friends.

Despite all the achievements, she wanted more. She set out to do the first solo flight from Hawaii to California through the Pacific Ocean, a route where many had lost their lives. She also flew from Los Angeles to Mexico City and New Jersey, where a crowd filled the runway to welcome her like a rock star.

The biggest challenge for Amelia was to circle the planet alongside the equator and achieve the longest distance ever flown. With a new aircraft, a Lockheed Electra 10, she took off from Los Angeles on May 27, 1939, accompanied by Fred Noonan, a navigator. They made their first stop in Florida, then continued on to Brazil. The next leg of their journey would lead them across the Atlantic Ocean and Africa, where they made their fourth stop. Amelia and Fred would go on to fly from the Red Sea to India, setting a new record. Everything was proceeding smoothly until they reached Java Island in Indonesia. The aircraft suffered some damage, the weather was less than optimal, and Amelia got sick with dysentery. Nevertheless, when they arrived in Australia, she felt so confident in their possibilities that she shipped the parachutes back to the U.S., as she thought they would not make use of them. On July 2, 1937, they took off from New Guinea to face the last part of their journey across the Pacific Ocean. The plane's signal got lost when they were flying in terrible weather over the Nukumanu Islands. President Roosevelt immediately sent a fleet to rescue them, but the search contingent was never able to find the crew or scraps of the plane.

They declared Amelia dead two years after her disappearance, on January 5, 1939. Eighty years had to go by for her remains to be identified. What until 2018 were thought to be the bones of a man found in 1940 on Nikumaroro Island were, in fact, Amelia's remains. Scientists were able to confirm the identity using new forensic methods to measure bones and extract information from the analysis.

Her tragic death only served to enhance her status as a legend at a time when women were mostly confined to the private sphere. In a letter she wrote to her husband that was to be opened in case of her death, she told him, "Women must try to do things as men have tried." Cheers to that.

Valentina Tereshkova: The Seagull of the Stars

Valentina Vladimirovna Tereshkova was born on March 6, 1937, in Bolshoye Maslennikovo, part of the Yaroslavl Oblast in Russia. At the time, the Union of Soviet Socialist Republics (USSR). Her family was formed by her grandmother, her parents —Vladimir and Elena Fyodorovna—her older sister and her younger brother. They had emigrated from Belarus before Valentina came into the world.

When she was only two years old, her father—a tractor driver—was conscripted to fight in World War II and died during combat in the Battle of Finland. Such tragedies were informed by telegram back then, and as children of the war, she and her siblings knew what it was to see their mother cry on a piece of paper. She was one of the millions who would repeat the scene until the end of the war.

Consequently, Elena found herself the sole breadwinner of the family, with three children all too young. She worked as a milkmaid and received 50 rubles per child as an allowance, but with a loaf of bread costing 200 rubles, it was hardly enough to get by. After the German army left in 1941, she decided to move to the capital of the Oblast, Yaroslavl, to look for a better life for her family. There, she found a job in a textile factory. Valentina later developed a very close relationship with her mother, whom she greatly admired for the strength she had shown while raising her children all by herself. It is said that in school, she would draw often.

In her childhood, the railway track sat very close to Valentina's home, and she would spend hours watching the train go by. This made her develop a desire to become a train driver as she grew up. The endless machine in front of her child's eyes seemed magical and like a ticket to visit distant lands and cities.

She entered school at the age of eight but dropped out at 16 to help the family earn an income. Regardless, she continued her education while working and graduated from the Light Industry Technical School in 1960.

Her job at the textile mill, alongside other young women, brought many friendships. The mill was by the riverbank, right in front of the local Voluntary Society for Assistance to the Army, Air Force, and Navy (DOSAAF) Aviation Club, where the women could see across the river people jumping off planes when they arrived at work and left.

Curiosity made Valentina start taking skydiving lessons. She was quite daring and learned very fast, which allowed her to attempt her first jump before turning 22. She was terrified, but when the moment came, she did not let her fear take over; she looked at the vastness of the sky and jumped forward. After that, she could never stop. And even though she was a very driven person, she did not get particularly good grades in her jumps, something that both frustrated and saddened her.

While working, she would listen to the radio daily. One auspicious day, she heard the news that young cosmonaut Yuri Gagarin had succeeded in completing a space flight around the planet. Arriving home, she told her mother the news, to which Elena replied that it was time for a woman to achieve the same. Another example of how surprising the paths of life can be.

Around this time, Valentina became secretary to the Komsomol, the All-Union Leninist Young Communist League, and thus began her political career. Two years later, she joined the Communist Party of the Soviet Union (CPSU).

With the space race raging between the US and the USSR, Air Force vice commander Nikolay Kamanin was appointed to the task of assembling the cosmonaut program. It was his idea to bring women into the program to study the effects of the flights on a female body, as well as on a male's. Valentina's selection on February 16, 1962, was due to her experience as a skydiver. Four hundred women made up the first batch of candidates, but only five remained in the final group.

Due to the highly classified status of the program, Valentina could not even tell Elena what she was doing or where she was, so she made up that she had been invited to be a reserve member of the U.S.S.R. parachuting team in Moscow. Training included zero-g-flights, isolation and centrifuge tests, rocket theory, spacecraft engineering, 120 parachute jumps, and pilot training in MiG-15UTI jet fighters. It was a thorough, several-month extreme training program with a final examination. So extreme that the force of the centrifuge would leave red spots on their skin due to the bursting of small blood vessels.

After the exam, the five women were offered a promotion from private to junior lieutenant in the Air Force. Sergei Korolev, the chief engineer for the program, supported Valentina due to her proletariat background and participation in politics. And so, out of the five, she was the chosen one. Valentina would later tell how Sergei became like a father to them.

On July 16, 1963, after all preparations were done, Valentina was ready to go for the stars. She put the space suit on and was transported by bus to the launch platform. As tradition goes, she emptied her bladder right on top of the bus tire. Heaven forbid something goes wrong. After testing all communication and life support devices, the door was sealed with her inside. Two hours later, the Vostok 6 was launched without major mechanical issues. Despite this, she did suffer from nausea and physical discomfort during most of the flight. The capsule orbited the Earth 48 times before coming back to the surface, which took three days to complete. During the trip, she took pictures of the horizon that would later be used for scientific research on atmospheric aerosols. Seagull was the nickname given to Valentina for the mission, which would stay with her to this day.

Once in orbit, the trajectory of the spacecraft had to be modified due to an error in calculations programmed in the ship's system. Thanks to the good work of Valentina and the team, she was able to eject from the capsule and come safely down to Earth after completing the mission. She landed 620 kilometers northeast of Karaganda, Kazakhstan, where the people living nearby offered her food. In return, she gave them the cosmonaut's food she had taken with her, something that would create a problem later, as the leftovers had to be counted and weighed to extract conclusions.

From that moment on, Valentina would hold innumerable political positions, both in domestic and international organizations. She was granted countless awards and recognitions for her contributions to women's advancement. From 1966 to 1974, she was a member of the Supreme Soviet, the year in which she ascended to a seat in the Presidium, a position she held until 1989 and the consequent fall of the Soviet Union. From 1969 to 1991, she was a member of the central committee of the Communist Party.

But one moment in Valentina's life felt to her like a gift from God. Or perhaps it was pity for her sick mother and her daughter. On a January morning in 1969, a delegation, including her, was to welcome a group of cosmonauts returning from a mission. They were heading in cars toward the Kremlin with a parade surrounding them. From the crowd, a man stepped forward and started shooting at one of the cars. The driver was killed during the incident, and nine bullets were later found on the side of the car where Valentina was sitting. She emerged unharmed. The target was Premier Leonid Brézhnev, but the shooter, Viktor Ilyin, made a mistake in choosing the target car. He was arrested on the spot and later declared insane.

On November 3rd, 1963, she got married to fellow cosmonaut Andriyan Nikolayev in a sumptuous wedding ceremony presided over by Khrushchev, and nearly a year later, she would give birth to their daughter, Elena Andrianovna Nikolaeva-Tereshkova, named after Valentina's loving mother. Unfortunately, Valentina and Andriyan were not made for each other, and the time came when they could not even be in the same room together. They finally filed for divorce in 1982. But love was not over for Valentina, and it took the form of a surgeon she met while reapplying for spaceflight in 1978. She waited four years to marry Yuli Shaposhnikov.

Valentina began her Space Engineering studies at the Zhukovsky Air Force Engineering Academy while training for the Vostok mission, where she graduated with honors in 1969. Eight years later, she got her Ph.D. in Aeronautical Engineering. In 1997, having reached the legal age, she retired from the Air Force and the Cosmonaut Corps with the rank of Colonel. Two years later, Yuli passed away. Happily, she has her daughter and two grandsons accompanying her in life.

Even though Valentina flew into space only once, her deed inspired dreams in countless young people, especially young girls, who look up to her and learn that not only men can achieve the greatest goals. She remains active in politics to this day and is considered a heroine in Russia.

Bessie Coleman: Flying to Be Free

Elizabeth Coleman was born on January 26th, 1892, in Atlanta, Texas. Bessie was only one of thirteen siblings. Sadly, it was commonplace for families to lose babies at the time, and they lost four. The infant mortality rate was much higher than it is today, especially among black and indigenous groups. Both her parents were African-American, and her father was of Cherokee ancestry.

A small cabin in Waxahachie—a town almost 300 km south-west of Atlanta—accommodated the numerous family members; George and Susan had decided to move there two years after Bessie's birth. With dirt floors and a couple of square meters for 11, they were far from comfortable. Opportunities were scarce in those years, but despite difficulties, the children attended a segregated school.

To earn a living, the Colemans worked as sharecroppers. The older children, including Bessie, would help their mother pick cotton when the harvest season arrived. But life as a farmer was too hard for George, and some years later, he left his family to pursue better prospects in Oklahoma.

Bessie stood out as a student, which led to her being granted a scholarship at the Missionary Baptist Church School at age 12. After graduation, she enrolled at the Oklahoma Colored Agricultural and Normal University in Langston but was only able to attend for a single semester before running out of money. She returned home, and it was not long before she made new plans. In 1915, Bessie packed her things and left for Chicago alongside millions of other African-Americans heading north to escape racial violence and find a better future.

To put her life in the proper historical context: The 1896

Supreme Court case Plessy vs. Ferguson—commonly known as the "Jim Crow laws"—had made legal the racial segregation black people were already suffering from. The year 1919 saw the breakout of a bloody racial war throughout the country. That summer was baptized the Red Summer. Lynchings and burns were at stake everywhere.

In a curiously similar scene with Amelia Earhart, Bessie would hear stories from pilots who had fought in World War I at her workplace—stories that convinced her she had been born to fly. After four years of working in a barber shop as a manicurist and at a restaurant, she started applying to flying schools around the country, but nobody would teach her. The current circumstances were against her desire; she was black and a woman. Nonetheless, she continued in her pursuit. She went to Robert Abbott, the owner of The Chicago Defender, to plead her case to him. He was left impressed after Bessie presented her arguments for a black woman to be allowed to fly and offered to sponsor her. In addition, he published her story in his newspaper, a gesture that helped her gain a second sponsorship, this time from Banker Jesse Binga.

The following year, she sailed for France. She had been studying French for some months and could finally enroll at an aviation school in a town in northern France called Le Crotoy. There, no one cared about who she was, her willingness to learn was the decisive factor. She was in love with flying, and the time spent in France only served as confirmation.

In June 1921, she finally got her international flying license from the Fédération Aéronautique Internationale. She was the first black pilot—man or woman—with an international license.

Unlike Amelia, Bessie had, maybe, been born too soon. While Amelia was being paid to advertise commercial flights, even though she was not a commercial pilot herself, Bessie's only choice to make a living was barnstorming. Returning to the US, she would become a celebrity as a barnstormer. The highly risky entertainment had people fascinated all across the country. It included stunts performed mid-flight by civil pilots individually or in groups, such as walking on the planes' wings, jumping from planes, and doing extreme figures. But before launching into the flying show business, she had to spend another four or so months undergoing intensive training in Europe. Yet again, nobody in her country wanted to teach her.

Her fame and travels around the nation allowed her to take a stand against racism. Among her principles, she refused to perform in shows where black people were not allowed to use the front entrance. Given the circumstances, she could have just stayed silent, but her compassionate nature would not let her sit by. She hated the idea of other black people having to suffer what she suffered. To do that, she decided to open a flying school for black people, particularly black women. Well aware of the symbolic power she held, she intended to train her replacement in case something were to happen to her, be it an accident or something else.

In 1923, Bessie purchased her very own plane. A month later, bad luck caught up with her, and she crashed near Santa Monica, California. With great luck, she was pulled out of the wreckage alive with only a broken leg and ribs. From the hospital bed, she promised to come back. And two years later, she made her long-awaited comeback with a tour around Texas, her hometown included. Seeing all the people proud of her and cheering for her felt like the success she had been looking for.

On April 30th, 1926, during preparations for a show in Jacksonville, Florida, Bessie was violently thrown from a plane at 600 meters to her death. Her mechanic, William Wills, who was flying the device, also died instantly when the plane crashed to the ground. The tragedy shocked the country, with newspapers informing us that The Only Race Aviatrix in the World had died. She was 34 years old. The plane was a recent purchase and had

had deficient maintenance before the flight test. And though Bessie was aware, she refused to fly another aircraft.

The aviation school she had dreamed of finally became a reality in 1929 when her friend and colleague William Powell founded the Bessie Coleman Aeroclub.

Even though she died young, she has remained a figure of strength ever since. Bessie was not only an inspiration for black women, but she also inspired black men to become pilots. The Tuskegee Airmen of World War II were among them. The group would honor her yearly by flying over her grave to drop flowers.

HOW TO USE VISION AND DIRECTION TO BUILD RESILIENCE

In Aviation and any other form of transport, having a destination before the commencement of the journey is crucial. If an itinerary was not set beforehand for trains and planes, there would be chaos.

The same is true for us. Setting a destination at the start of the journey is one important aspect, but adjusting the plan to avoid stormy weather along the way is equally important. If we face challenges and difficulties, we might need to slightly adjust our journey, but it is easier to navigate through hurdles and barriers and get back on the right path when we know where we are headed.

By creating a clear vision of the destination, our dreams, and our ideas, we set the course. Obstacles along the way are inevitable and expected, especially when we are trying something new, but with vision, we can set the course and stay the course.

Visualizing is the keyword to introduce. The meaning may appear straightforward, but it is not as easy as it sounds; it takes practice, focus, repetition, and a strong will. Sometimes, it even requires outside support to stay true to our vision. When we know, feel, and visualize our destination, *how* to get there will be shown to us as soon as we move in the right direction.

Continuing to dream and visualize your vision will eventually cause small and big ideas to come to you that will guide you to the next step of action on the path of achieving your dream; possibilities that were not there before or perhaps were just invisible to you, suddenly become clear. It feels as if the circle of circumstances enclosing and holding you captive becomes brittle and cracks appear, letting light through for you to see an open window of opportunity.

All of this was true for our three protagonists in the chapter. Although their circumstances were nothing to their advantage, they saw themselves up in the air, and that is where they eventually went.

Amelia faced difficult circumstances when her father lost his job, and her grandmother passed away. She later volunteered as a nurse. But what happened then? She found her vision when she heard the stories of heroic pilots. Life, giving her a second chance—the first she had ignored as a child—presented that vision for her to hold onto. And she did. She lived a life full of detours but with a fixed destination. So fixed that she even lost her life pursuing her vision.

Valentina's journey is in some aspects similar to Amelia's. A woman in a difficult economic situation, working to make ends meet and finding a vision in the meantime. A vision that seemed more than impossible for a woman at the time and in her situation. Adjusting the course of life while obstacles or opportunities presented themselves, but never leaving the vision of the skies aside.

For Bessie, I would like to focus on the vision she had for an aviation school for black people, free from discrimination. She could not see it through herself, but it became a reality nonetheless. So strong was her vision that even her loving friends were impacted by it.

Vision, Direction, and Circumstances

Do you define circumstances, or do circumstances define you? In other words, do you let facts and circumstances determine who you are? It is easy to fall into the so-called "victim role" if you believe that you are unable to create your own circumstances. Our goal is to change that mindset and take up a role of action, controlling our own lives while acknowledging that there are circumstances in life we cannot control, but they do not have to define us; they are just part of us and our journey.

If we were to see the world through a lens, it might feel as if we are standing alone in a vast space with negative circumstances surrounding us; we might feel trapped and helpless with no way out. But that is not the truth; there is always a way out of circumstances. It is how we control our reaction to such events that makes the difference. It is about shifting our focus from feeling stuck and encircled in current circumstances to visualizing what we want to experience.

The trick with focus is that when we put our attention on something, it subconsciously becomes our intention. We have all heard the saying, "Don't think about a pink elephant," and although we were not thinking about it before, we suddenly cannot stop thinking about it now. The same principle applies to the challenging circumstances in our lives. Because we are focusing too much on what we do not want, we end up getting more of exactly that.

Small Exercise to Define Your Vision and Grow Resilience

- A question to ask ourselves is: What would we love to experience instead of our current circumstances? What would we like to see if we had a magic wand? What would our new chosen reality look like? And most importantly, how would this chosen dream feel, or how would we feel in this vision?

- Close your eyes and visualize your dream in all its details, including colors, smells, and sensations.
- Write it down with all the details but use the present tense as if it were already a reality. Start the sentence with gratitude: "I am so grateful now that I...."
- For the moment, you do not have to know how to get there; just feel as if you have already achieved your dream.
- Read your dream to yourself every morning and every evening for at least 90 days.
- Initially, the shift begins within your emotional state before it is noticeable in your cognitive state. But pay attention to how circumstances change and how new doors begin to open for you.

5

BUILDING OUR COURAGE

Courage is not the absence of fear, it is the ability to act in the presence of fear. –Bruce Lee

INTRODUCTION

How many fiction stories in the history of humanity have been written with courage as their main theme? Curiously, there were mostly men at the center and as subjects performing the courageous deeds. Women were merely objects of desire or the element to save. To challenge this notion, let me share a quote by Jane Austen: "There is a stubbornness about me that never can bear to be frightened at the will of others. My courage always rises at every attempt to intimidate me" (1813, p. 122).

In this chapter, I aim to make women the subjects performing the courageous deeds by telling the stories of very real and impressive women—all from different eras and sides of the world—within the industry of medicine, one where we must be brave when faced with emergencies. We will learn how they courageously tackled challenges to achieve their dreams.

Following the previous chapter's theme, it is time to see our vision through with courage, despite the possibility of facing one's worst fears.

What Constitutes Courage?

What is courage? And sometimes called bravery or valor.

It is defined by our friendly dictionary (Merriam-Webster, 2009) as follows: "Mental or moral strength to venture, persevere, and withstand danger, fear, or difficulty." Reads simple.

Here we give another definition from the APA Dictionary (American Psychological Association, n.d.-b), perhaps a more accurate one: "The ability to meet a difficult challenge despite the physical, psychological, or moral risks involved in doing so. Examples of acts of courage include saving another's or one's own life against a meaningful threat; coping with a painful, debilitating, or terminal illness; overcoming a destructive habit; and voicing an unpopular opinion."

What these previous definitions fail to mention is that it is a *choice*.

We can then distinguish two categories: Physical and moral courage. The first refers to the choice to face the eventuality of pain or death for a greater purpose, and the second is the choice to act rightly at the risk of facing shame, scandal, discouragement, or personal loss.

Professor Daniel Putman talks about courage needing a balance between fear and self-confidence in order to achieve a worthy goal. Too much fear and you will never face risky circumstances; too much self-confidence, and you will overstretch your own skills and abilities when facing danger.

Florence Nightingale: A Mathematician's Creativity at the Service of Health

Born on May 12, 1820, in Florence, Italy, Florence—quite evidently named after the city where she was born—was the second daughter of a wealthy British family. William and Frances Nightingale were on an extended European tour at the time. With a privileged upbringing full of language classes, mathematics courses, and discussions about philosophy, but also strict and restrictive, her parents expected her to marry well; she was very educated but only in the roles of wife and mother, regardless of her own desires.

Despite her parents' expectations, Florence found her calling —she was a devoted Christian—to pursue a different path in life. As a young woman, she asked them to let her study mathematics first and nursing later. The couple refused, as nursing was considered lowly and disreputable. She would have to wait 14 years—and reject a problematic suitor—for them to finally let her leave for Germany to take a two-week course at a nursing hospital. She was 30 years old.

After some years of training and working at the Hospital for Distressed Gentlewomen in London, in 1854, Florence was asked to lead a team of nurses to care for British soldiers who had been wounded in the Crimean War—a conflict that left an estimate of one million lives lost—during the fall of the Ottoman Empire. The conditions in the military hospital of Scutari were appalling, with inadequate food and water, scarce medical supplies, and a high mortality rate due to infectious diseases. The sewer waters would flood the place, and ventilation was non-existent. Therefore, Florence and her team resolved to work tirelessly to improve the situation, often at great personal risk. She became known as the "Lady With the Lamp," as she would make nightly rounds of the hospital wards, carrying a lamp to comfort and care for the sick and injured.

During her time in Crimea, she fell ill with Brucellosis; the bacterial disease nearly killed her. And even though she recovered, the infection would come to haunt her later in life.

Florence's efforts in the war made her a national hero in Britain upon her arrival in 1856. She became a tireless advocate for healthcare reform, using her knowledge of math and statistics. She lobbied the government—presenting the Coxcomb Graph, now widely used to show data visually—to improve sanitary conditions in hospitals and to properly train nurses. By the beginning of the 1860s, the reforms had been implemented all across Britain, proving the efficacy of her plan.

The infection she had picked up in Crimea would come back in 1857. She suffered a collapse and had to live the rest of her life between bed and a bit of the outside world. But that would not stop her from founding the Nightingale Training School for Nurses at St. Thomas' Hospital in London in 1860, which became a model for nursing education around the world. It would not be long before nursing schools were multiplying everywhere, thanks to the numerous women Florence mentored.

In her bed, she wrote innumerable letters to advocate for policies on equal access to healthcare, books, and treatises on nursing and public health. But she despised fame, even expressing the desire to be forgotten once she passed away. We are not being respectful of her desires, but hopefully, it is for a good cause.

Florence died on August 13th, 1910, at the age of 90. She dedicated her life to the profession, even to the detriment of her own social connections, with only one other woman known to have been a friend. It can be said that she was married to her career and passion at a time when such bravery was only a man's deed.

Betsi Cadwaladr: From Underdog to Courageous Leader

Elizabeth Cadwaladr was born in the rural Welsh village of Llanycil on May 24, 1789. Betsi—as she was usually called—was one of the daughters of a very numerous family dedicated to farming; sixteen children, to be precise. Her father, Dafydd, was a Christian preacher. Very soon in life, she experienced a vital loss when her mother passed away. She was five years old. Because of this, the responsibility of the household fell on her older sister.

As so many of the women in this book experienced in their lives, Betsi's turning point in hers was when she got her hands on a Bible; those pages gave her purpose.

Her fiery spirit and independent nature would make her leave the family's house at age nine due to disagreements with her sister. That spirit would arise again, but this time, to disagree with another notable woman from this book: Florence Nightingale.

For a farm girl at that time who did not speak English, one of the few options for work and education was to become a maid. During her time working as a teacher at Plas Yn Dre, she learned English and music. That would not last long, either, and five years later, she left for Liverpool. Over the next few years, she went back to Wales and left again, refusing to get married.

Her nursing calling did not come until much later. In the years after her move to London, she worked as an assistant to many different people and in many different places. One of these was the Battle of Waterloo, a tragic day in 1815 that left a great impression on her. Especially significant were her times aboard ships. In these, she had the opportunity—and blessing—to visit much of the world and to make acquaintances with notable people, which broadened her perspectives. She was also pushed by circumstances to help in ways she had not anticipated, tending to the sick.

Little is known about Betsi's time at a London Hospital after her return from the sea, where she trained as a nurse.

In 1854, she joined the group of women sent to Crimea by the British government to assist in the conflict. That is when the problems with Florence began; the English nurse had strong disagreements with Betsi. They were both strong-willed women. The bureaucracy of Florence's method frustrated her, leading her to ignore the rules when she thought they were useless. But the most important difference between the women working at Scutari was class. Florence, coming from a wealthy background (as did many of her nurses), did not require payment. Betsi, on the other hand, needed a salary to support herself, which added to the bad reputation of the profession. The other factor that contributed to Florence's rejection of Betsi was that she was Welsh. Part of the reason for this rejection was a publication by the British government a few years before; the Reports of the Commissioners of Inquiry into the State of Education in Wales of 1847—more commonly called the Blue Books—questioned the religion, the language, and the morals of the Welsh people. The Blue Books were seen as slander, something that infuriated them and contributed to the mutual rejection of English and Welsh.

After many arguments, Betsi decided to transfer to Balaclava, where she asked the commander-in-chief to support her in her disagreement with Florence. What to some might only be disrespect, given her station, to others was an act of courage. And it was worth it. In no time, she was managing seven wards and the diet kitchen. The work was grueling; the days were 18 hours, seven days a week.

How the two women approached caring for the wounded

could not have been more different. While Florence did not allow her nurses to go near the wounded men after dark and were forbidden from speaking to them, Betsi advocated for more humane and loving care.

Betsi's health would eventually deteriorate; she fell ill with cholera and dysentery and was forced to go back to Britain. She was 65 at the time.

She dedicated the last years of her life to her autobiography and spending time with her sister. She died in 1860 at the age of 71.

If Florence had introduced numbers into patient care, Betsi introduced compassion. She remains a symbol of the strong will of the Welsh people and an example for her country.

Fe Del Mundo: Simple Solutions to Complicated Problems

Fé Primitiva del Mundo y Villanueva was born on November 27, 1911, in Manila, Philippines. Her parents were lawyers Bernardo del Mundo and Paz Villanueva. At the time, the family lived in downtown Manila, in a place called Intramuros—meaning *inside the walls*—where only important people had a home.

She was the fifth of eight children. It can be seen how many of these remarkable women shared events in their lives. Fe shared the loss of three baby siblings and her eleven-year-old sister Elisa with Bessie Coleman. Before her death from appendicitis, Elisa had expressed to Fe her intention of becoming a doctor. Though tragedy prevented her from doing so, Fe would make that desire her own. Shortly after her sister's death, she suffered another loss, this time her mother. She was 14 years old.

Fe had always shown a passion for learning, and this, together with the pain and frustration that stemmed from seeing children being buried more often than adults in her community, made her apply for a medical degree. In 1926, she entered the College of Medicine at the University of the Philippines. But those were hard times; her father could not support her financially. Much to her—and later, patients of hers—luck, a loving aunt offered the needed support. By 1933, she had graduated at the top of her class with a medical degree in pediatrics and passed the medical board exam.

A few years after her graduation, President Manuel Quezon offered to pay for her further education at any university she chose in the US. Thus, it is said she became the first Asian female student at Harvard, but this has been contested since Harvard Medical School did not allow women students until 1945. What she did instead—as she already had a medical degree —was work as an assistant physician at the Boston Children's Hospital. This position allowed her to complete graduate work at Harvard Medical School. She then went on to work at the University of Chicago, Johns Hopkins Hospital, and other institutions.

After completing her studies at Harvard and the Boston University School of Medicine in 1941—with a master's degree in bacteriology under her arm—Fe returned to the Philippines, just in time to witness her country being invaded by Imperial Japan. She was living with her sister's family at the time.

Seeing the conflict unfold, she did not hesitate to join the International Red Cross. Her work comprised taking care of children who were prisoners of war in an internment camp at the University of Santo Tomas. She convinced the Japanese officials to let her take the children from the camp to a children's home, where they would be better-taken care of. Four hundred little souls were treated by her during the occupation. And just like Florence Nightingale earned her nickname because of her dedicated work, so did Fe: The Angel of Santo Tomas.

With the war going strong by 1943—and it would get even stronger—the mayor of Manila asked Fe to be director of a children's hospital and later a full-scale medical center, where she would remain head until 1948. Fe always had a sweet spot for children. Her niece remembers how she would take her to do rounds to patients' homes as a child.

She founded the Children's Medical Center Foundation in 1957, quickly becoming one of Southeast Asia's leading pediatric hospitals. She also established the Institute of Maternal and Child Health, which provided training and education for healthcare professionals throughout the region.

But the story behind the Medical Center's establishment is as curious as it is remarkable. She sold her family home and most of her belongings and took out a loan to finance the construction. From that moment on, she lived on the hospital's second floor.

Medical practice was not her only interest. She would remain committed to advancing the field of pediatrics in the Philippines and improving the lives of children. For this reason, she joined the University of Santo Tomas and became head of the Department of Pediatrics. In the fields of research, she dedicated her time to infectious diseases like dengue, polio, and measles and published the first textbook–*Textbook of Pediatrics and Child Health*–on pediatrics authored by a Filipino.

Creativity and simple solutions were her trademarks. So much so that in 1973, she designed a ground-breaking, low-cost incubator made of bamboo that could be used in rural areas and to which a fluorescent light could be attached to treat babies suffering from jaundice. This link between health institutions and the extended community she was a part of was the most important aspect of her teaching.

Fe passed away on August 6, 2011, at the age of 99, still doing morning rounds in a wheelchair in her beloved hospital. She was never married, nor did she have children of her own, but it can be said that by acting as a motherly figure for many children in need throughout her life, she became the mother of a nation.

Paulina Luisi: Politics and Medicine

Paulina Luisi was born on December 23, 1875, in Colón, Entre Ríos, Argentina. She was one of eight children from the marriage of Angel Luisi and María Teresa Josefina Janicki. Angel was an Italian lawyer from Pisa, and Josefina came from a Polish family exiled to France. Josefina, being a professor with a degree from the Sorbonne, was a great influence on Paulina and her siblings. Moreover, she was part of the suffragette movement in France before moving with her husband to Argentina in 1873.

The couple founded a liberal school upon their arrival in Argentina—the *Escuela Moderna*—but shortly after, they decided to relocate to Paysandú, Uruguay. Continuing with the tradition, they set up a similar school in their new city and dedicated themselves fully to the education field. Given the egalitarian treatment the parents dispensed to their children, they decided to send their daughters to a boarding school in Montevideo to become schoolteachers.

Paulina started working immediately after her graduation. But her mind demanded more, and in 1900, she decided to study medicine at the University of the Republic of Uruguay. At the time, it was not illegal for women to go to university but in practice, not a single one attended medical school before Paulina. So strange her presence there was that her classmates would often play jokes on her. One memorable time, someone slipped a corpse's male genitalia in her medical coat's pocket, expecting a scene for reaction, but got only disappointment when she wittily replied by asking who had lost a penis.

She graduated in 1908 as Uruguay's first female physician, and from that moment on, she expanded her connections by writing to and engaging with the Argentinian feminists of the time, the *Universitarias*—Petrona Eyle, Alicia Moreau de Justo, Sara Justo, and Julieta Lanteri, among many others. Their discussions were centered on two main topics: How to improve the living conditions of women and how to legalize the female vote. They held their first meeting—the International Feminine Congress—in Buenos Aires in 1910.

Politics was always Paulina's passion, and that was made apparent when she helped found the Uruguayan Socialist Party. From that platform, she linked her other two passions— teaching and medicine—to advocate for sex-health education in secondary schools—a change that would wait until 1944 to be implemented. She was undoubtedly ahead of her time. So ahead of time, being the first female doctor brought praise, but it also brought questioning. How could she possibly examine men? For this reason, she was forced to continue working as a teacher and in the Department of Obstetrics-Gynecology at the University.

While fully immersed in the politics of the capital, she met President José Batlle y Ordoñez, who offered to award a grant for her to study social hygiene—the practice of measures aiming at the elimination of venereal disease and prostitution to protect and improve the family as a social institution (Merriam-Webster)—in France. There, she completed postgraduate studies in dermatology and venereal diseases. And just like her mother did decades earlier, she became acquainted with the French suffragettes, in particular with Madame Bonnevial, a prominent activist for the eradication of the slave sex trade— formerly known as the white slave sex trade.

Upon her return to Montevideo, Paulina resolved to set up her own medical practice, a position that allowed her to frequent the intellectual elite of Uruguayan politics. With these connections, she formed the National Women's Council, a branch of the International Council of Women. The most important step they took to advance women's rights came when the Council presented a project to establish women's right to vote to the constitutional assembly in 1916. Due to a lack of support from the male members of the parties involved, they failed to change the constitution.

In the following years, she helped found two working women's trade unions, the Women Alliance for Women's Rights—affiliated with the International Woman Suffrage Alliance—and traveled to Europe to reunite with her feminist friends.

By 1922, Paulina was acting as a delegate of the Uruguayan government to the League of Nations Commission for the Protection of Children and Youth. Her work during that decade would also include other major international events.

In 1932, when women's suffrage was finally approved, she was in Madrid. In her congratulatory words to her fellow militants, she stated the need to advocate for the vote all across Latin America, a plan that would be interrupted by a coup d'etát a few months later.

Following the political turmoil in Uruguay, she decided to stay in Europe and would remain there for several years, well into the Spanish Civil War, where she supported the resistance.

After her return, she spent her time writing abolitionist theory—a subject to which she was a fervent supporter—and many more texts dedicated to her interests. During this time, she was lovingly given the nickname *La Abuela*—the grandmother—by her younger fellow militants.

On July 16, 1950, Uruguay was playing the final match of that year's Football World Cup against host and likely winner Brazil. Beating all odds, the Uruguayans won the title—an event called *Maracanazo* by the sport's fans. Paulina passed away on this very happy day for her country at the age of 74.

Interestingly, the word courage contains the Latin word for heart *cor*, so we can say it is our innermost feeling. It is the result of staying true to one's values and essence.

Within our hearts, strengths come from our passions, our values, and our beliefs, and these strengths enable us to muster up the courage to act with righteousness and face pain and fear. We need that courage to take the first step when fear is upon us. This might be what Goethe's most infamously attributed quote (even though it is not his) is referring to: "Be bold and mighty forces will come to your aid." The actual quote is "Go at it boldly, and you'll find unexpected forces closing around you and Coming to your aid." (King, 1921, p. 11).

But courage for what? The courage to stand up for others, for a community, and take courageous action for the greater good. And last but not least, to stand up for ourselves. We cannot expect it to be easy, but the first step is to believe a change can be made; it is getting into the mental space necessary to face difficulties, regardless of (self-)doubt and fear.

It is important to understand what fear represents to us: Nothing more than an indication whenever we leave our comfort zone. It is a reminder for us to never lose sight of the possibility that we might get hurt if we leave known territory and, at the same time, an invitation to come back to our comfort zone. But staying there permanently does not bring any opportunity for growth. In fact, if we never attempt to *live a life* in the presence of fear, never putting our courage into action, that fear takes over our lives, and the resulting avoidant behaviors make our comfort zone smaller and smaller until we cannot even move. We effectively become *paralyzed by fear*.

In the animal kingdom, some mammals show us how to prepare to overcome fear, especially big cats, and bears. They have developed an intimidating roar, signaling they are ready to face the challenge and gauging strength, putting their bodies into biochemical readiness to fight.

In movies, we often witness the moment the hero decides not to give up and bundles all their energy and strength to take courageous actions.

We can feel that in ourselves as well—an internal roar, going all in with all we have. I certainly did that when I found myself on exam day, almost frozen and crying at the bottom of the first-floor stairs of the hospital exam rooms. I was terrified of failing again, but with a little support from my mentor on the phone, I bundled up all I had, telling myself, "I am going to do this; I am going to show them I can do this." It instantly gave me this feeling of quiet confidence in my skills and abilities.

For the next three hours, I flew through the exam stations. For the first time in a long time, I felt like I was in control. And a few months later, when the results came out, I was not even surprised to have passed. Not only had I passed, but I had passed with a result that was significantly above the cut-off score. This was possible because I was able to control my fear and act with courage. Courage shifted my focus from "I don't want to fail" to "I am passing this exam; I can do this: bring it on! I am ready."

For the women in this chapter, the courage they showed in the face of the worst possible circumstances—war—life could present was the fuel they needed to overcome difficulties. They were not fearless; they took their fear and redirected it toward the greater good. They had the values and the vision, so they pursued their passion, and in following the set direction, the path was presented in due time. Why were they able to do it? Because they had faith.

As a final idea for this section, I want to share the following: Courage is needed to take action despite fear, and action is the antidote for fear. Getting to courage means walking through your vulnerability, including all your past failures.

Before we focus on the exercise, I would like to take you on a journey with my dear colleague and friend, Dr. Becc, in which she tells us about having the courage to stay true to our values and vision in the face of our conflicting sense of obligation about what we *should* do.

Rebecca Nothrop: Working for Other Women

Courage to stay true to oneself is equally important as courage to stand up for others. It is easy for personalities that are prone to work in medicine—female, altruistic, caring—to forget about themselves and focus solely on the well-being of others, fulfilling their expectations of who and how they apparently should be. Often, upbringing and cultural background play a role in how people prioritize the daily demands of life.

Dr. Rebecca Nothrop works as a coach to develop self-expression and self-assertiveness for women in medicine. She tells a wonderful story about us and our drive to care, contribute, and do the *right* thing. With this, however, she has seen a common dilemma arise: The compelling sense of obligation that ambitious, contentious women feel can have them deprioritize their own mission without their awareness.

She shares part of her story as follows:

For the caring, conscientious, and highly capable doctors I work with, it is common to see their navigation systems hijacked by "shoulds." These "shoulds" are the unwritten obligations—unplanned road maps—for our days.

The process looks something like this: We get into our cars each morning with an intention in mind for what will be our personal, meaningful destination. Topped up with fuel, we start driving towards that destination, be it nobly practicing medicine, being a loving, present parent or partner, practicing what

81

we preach—taking care of our health—or whatever is important to *us*. We are enlivened and determined by the thought of our destination. And we are willing to do the work to get there and make a difference.

But as our trip progresses on our daily drive to our destination, we pick up "passengers." They, too, have places they want to go and ideas about what matters. They sit in the passenger seat and authoritatively tell us where we are driving next.

These passengers are our "shoulds." They are the sentences of obligation that appear in our minds and derail us on our drive to our meaningful destination. Under the relentless demands of these "shoulds," we swerve, we detour, we speed up, and we slow down. At the end of the day, the gasoline light turns on, yet we have not made it to our destination. Again. And even if we could use our old, faithful grit and willpower to top up on fuel again, we are out of time.

You are not alone in feeling like your well-intended missions in life get hijacked.

The most common regret before dying is this: I wish I had dared to live a life true to myself rather than the one others expected of me.

I want you to remember that you all have fast and powerful cars. You have the skills and the sense of service to make a big difference in our world, not just as a carer for patients but as leaders for women everywhere, as well as in your personal lives and communities. Every day, you need to express and assert where you do and do not drive because if you do not prioritize your route—your life—your passengers will.

Now let's get fully into the exercises:

- Write a list of your strengths, talents, and skills.
  Follow it with a list of achievements in your life. You are more resourceful than you think. Write it down in your journal.

- Break out of your routine; do something new every day: e.g., take a different way to work, try a new recipe when cooking a meal, order something different in a restaurant or choose a new place for a meal, talk to a person you have never talked to before, or learn something new. The moment you feel worried and anxious about breaking out of your routine, visualize and remember the long list of your strengths.

I will take you on a little journey of reflection. Be open and let your mind take over while you are reading this:

- Take a moment and reflect upon all the "shoulds" in your life, as my colleague Dr. Northrop taught us.
- Make a mental note every time you use the words "I should be doing this." Notice how disempowering it is, minimizing our strength and making us feel out of control. The thought is hijacking our will from learning our true potential and increasing our fear of failing when we do not get all the shoulds done.
- Listen to your inner voice about what you would rather be doing, and have the courage to be true to yourself. Then think about one of the shoulds on your list. Maybe it is something like: "I should get the groceries today after work." Reflect on the following: Why is it a "should"? What would you rather be doing? Going to the movies? Reading a book? Then think of the reason why is it important to get the grocery shopping done today? Do you need food to feed your family? Is there something special that you want to get today? Or are there other options? For example, could you order the shopping online and have it delivered so you can use that time for other things, such as reading a book? And when you reflect

upon this now, did you have a choice? Did you choose one, the other, or both? How does it feel when you say, "I chose to do the grocery shopping today" instead of "I should"? Does it feel like being in control, like being in charge? What about the anxiety of failure? Of not getting it done and at the same time neglecting your own needs? When you practice more and more to stand up for yourself, you will also train the muscle of courage for other things.

6

CREATING A NETWORK OF SUPPORT

Our prime purpose in this life is to support others. And if you can't help them, at least don't hurt them. –H.H. Dalai Lama

INTRODUCTION

Much of the psychological work this book intends to focus on involves individual work. But humans are social creatures, and we thrive in the presence of our friends, families, and communities.

In the past, we began to develop ever bigger social networks —or political structures, from families to empires—to give answers to the needs of ever more complex humans. We must understand, first and foremost, that our vulnerabilities as animals are compensated by our ability to *flock*.

When we speak lately about societal *oppressions*, we do not speak as much about *freedoms*. One example: Would we be sharing this piece of writing if we had not set up rules for the symbols on this screen for everyone to learn and use? We build on what our ancestors did and thought. And even if we take the *selfish* approach, supporting others will eventually help us.

Let's dive into the concepts and the lives of women who support their force of life.

Support as Social Necessity

For our purposes, the definitions from Merriam-Webster (2018) for support are as follows:

- "To keep from fainting, yielding, or losing courage: comfort."
- "The act or process of supporting: the condition of being supported."

The APA Dictionary (2020) gives a more accurate and varied definition:

- "Social support: the provision of assistance or comfort to others, typically to help them cope with biological, psychological, and social stressors. Support may arise from any interpersonal relationship in an individual's social network involving family members, friends, neighbors, religious institutions, colleagues, caregivers, or support groups. It may take the form of practical help (e.g., doing chores, offering advice), tangible support that involves giving money or other direct material assistance, and emotional support that allows the individual to feel valued, accepted, and understood."

This definition tells us that support comes from a network that shares the same values among its members. And support is the fuel for the overall strategy we discuss in this book and the fire that encourages us never to give up.

One important concept I wish to present is that we have a

choice when taking comments or criticism because they can either be positive or negative. We must learn to discern between constructive criticism from those who have our best interests at heart and negative, destructive comments designed only to hurt us for whatever reason. Some feedback is necessary to help us improve and grow through those vulnerabilities that are not always apparent to our own eyes.

There are different types of support and aspects to the definition:

- Moral support can be the one parents give children when they are learning to decide what is "right" and what is "wrong." So we can say it involves contributing only with emotional or psychological encouragement.
- Peer support refers to a specific type of social support provided by an *equal*. We can say, in this case, that the relationship established is organized in a horizontal hierarchy.
- Sympathy serves us to perceive, understand, and react to the suffering or needs of other life forms.

Philosopher David Hume argues that sympathy arises when an individual switches from a personal to a social perspective in order to attend to another individual who is in need or lacking. Just like diseases are transported from human to human, so are emotions. This is justified by the notion that all minds are functionally similar.

And professor Brené Brown defines sympathy as a way to stay out of touch with one's emotions.

Sympathy is part of our evolution; it is a factor in social intelligence and the evolution of humanity. It is also linked to cognitive skills and communication, and empathy is the earliest form of sympathy.

In simple terms, sympathy means "I understand what you feel," but it keeps me at a distance from the suffering of another individual. Empathy, in turn, means "I feel the same as you do, even without being in the same situation." The power of empathy is that it binds me with this other individual by going into their emotions and feeling them together.

One of the fields where support—particularly emotional support—is essential is sports. Fans are literally called supporters. Since the performance is intricately woven with the emotional state of the sportsperson, cheering or the knowledge that people are backing them propels them forward.

The stories of the women in this chapter fit perfectly; they all thrived in the fields of sports.

SUPPORT IN SPORTS AND THE WOMEN WHO SHAPED HISTORY

Alice Milliat: Alice in Sportsland

This next fighter for the rights of women, named Alice Joséphine Marie Million, was born in Nantes, France, on May 5, 1884. The family made a living in the grocery business, and later, her father—Hippolyte—went to work at an office and her mother—Joséphine—at a sewing workshop. Alice was the eldest of five children.

As a young girl, Alice would read Alice in Wonderland— there was something there, no doubt—and the newspapers her father brought home. Unlike most girls her age and time, she practiced sports, mainly swimming and hockey. The conventions of the time were that women were only allowed to do physical exercises designed to enhance their capability to bear children. Those girls' mothers were in charge of restraining their daughters' urges to jump, run, and climb.

In 1896, in Athens, Greece, the first modern Olympic Games

took place. Faithful to her habits, she was closely following the results of her compatriots. It was an all-men competition, a striking thing that led her to wonder why there were no women. By the next edition of the games, which were to take place in Paris, people were already questioning the non-existing presence of women in the competition.

But the absence of women was not the only problem these first editions of the games showed. The competition was designed to enable only rich young amateur *gentlemen* to participate, as they were the only ones who could afford to take time from their studies.

The man behind the organization of the Games was a Baron by the name of Pierre de Coubertin. He was responsible for the lack of women competing; it was his belief that women should only be dedicated to the home and the children. Nonetheless, he allowed women to compete in two disciplines: golf and tennis. The following editions saw very little progress.

During her secondary school years, she trained as a teacher, a diploma she would put to good use a few years later. In 1904, Alice met businessman Joseph Milliat. They got married not long after and moved to England. There, she showed how much of a modern character she had, and proof of this was that she began working as a governess. It was in this land that she surrounded herself with other women who practiced sports, a fact that helped her grow a sense of companionship and purpose.

She continued to develop as an athlete and was determined to play her part in competitive sport, despite the prevailing societal and institutional—some unwritten, but many actually written—rules that stated women should not engage in such activities, instead, stay home, raise children, and cultivate femininity. Her main interests were track and field, rowing, hockey, and swimming.

Destiny had plans for her, and four years later, Joseph fell ill and passed away. They never had children, and not much more is known about their private lives. After her husband's death, she continued her travels around Europe. Immersing herself in other cultures helped her language skills develop further; some scholars even claim she spoke seven languages.

By the year 1912, Alice had become a member of the newly-formed club Fémina-Sport. It was her first approach to an institution dedicated to women's sports. In its early years, the club's main focus was gymnastics, following doctors' prescriptions. Later, during the war, athletics and team sports were introduced.

In 1913, she attended the International Women's Sports Congress/International Congress of Physical Education in Paris, where she advocated for the inclusion of women's sports in the Olympic Games. Her efforts were unsuccessful, as the International Olympic Committee (IOC) at the time did not believe women were capable of participating in such *virile* physical activities. At the beginning of her journey as a women's sports activist, she faced countless different institutionalized opinions and worked to reach accords between parties to achieve results. Some people favored breaking up with the IOC, while others were inclined more toward negotiating.

When the First World War broke out, she ended her travels and returned to France, but she was somewhat different. The ideas of the suffragettes were strong in England and had caught up with her. Given her skills, she volunteered as a translator. It was the women who held the fort during that time.

With the men off to war, the club organized its first athletic competition in 1917. The success made the members aim higher and founded the Fédération des Sociétés Féminines Sportives de France (FSFSF), an organization dedicated to promoting women's athletics. Alice was appointed to the Treasury. Two years later, she unanimously became its chairwoman. Such was the ability for leadership that she displayed.

Track and field were some of the sports Alice wished to include in the Olympic Games to be celebrated in 1924. The International Association of Athletics Federations (IAAF) replied negatively. She then had two options, give up or set up a Women's Olympiad of her own. Monte Carlo was the chosen spot. Ironically, she did not attend the 1921 event, even though she had worked hard to bring about the competition. The reasons point to a dispute with the French Athletics Federation (FFA) for the control of women's sports, but without significant change.

Consequently, Alice and other activists founded the Federation Sportive Feminine Internationale (FSFI), the equivalent international organization for women's sports. The FSFI organized its own Paris Women's Olympic Games, which were held in 1922 and attracted athletes from across Europe. The choice of city was not arbitrary; funny enough, it could be seen as a mockery of the Baron, who was from Paris. The dispute for the name—*Jeux Olympiques Féminins*, in French—saw an agreement when Belgian aristocrat Henri de Baillet-Latour—the Baron's successor to the IOC—offered to add ten women's events to the next edition of the Games. Then, the Women's Games held in Gothenburg, Sweden, in 1926 officially changed their name to the Women's World Games. But it would not end there, as Alice and the FSFI thought women's track and field events had to be included.

Among the many abilities Alice had, writing was one. Magazines and other publications were the platforms she used to spread her thoughts. When it came to activism, her style was incisive, straightforward, and charged with irony.

During those years, there were two main currents of opinion. One described as "egalitarian" sought equality between men and women in every sports practice, even if they needed to make some concessions with medical professionals. The other, commonly known as a "differentialist," sought to follow medical advice very precisely. The differentialist group followed the ideas of those who thought women needed to restrain themselves, as it was believed that more intense or competitive sports were negative for their bodies and reproductive capacities. Alice, on the other hand, advocated for the independence of women's sports institutions from men's and from men themselves, thus allowing women to make their own decisions regarding their practice of sports, but gave in to some medical recommendations of the time—many disregarded today—by easing the rules of the sports played by women, a move that enabled the Federation to keep the competitive sports (races, football, and rugby).

Alice's efforts finally paid off in 1928 when the IOC agreed to include five women's events in the Olympic Games in Amsterdam. She was instrumental in getting the events added, as she had organized a women's track and field competition in Paris the previous year that drew over 200 female athletes from around the world.

By 1934, she was tired of the half-achievements, and the circumstances led her to give an ultimatum, either the 1936 Olympics progress to fully integrate women or cede all women's events to the FSFI. It was a successful move. The program expanded, and the records set in the Women's Games were recognized.

Two years later, she decided to retire, passing the torch to the next generation. Despite the personal challenges she faced, she continued to be a passionate advocate for women's sports. She was a fixture at international sports events and worked tirelessly to ensure that women had the opportunity to compete on an equal footing with men.

Alice's work was not only focused on sports, however. She remained a feminist and believed that women should have equal rights in all aspects of society. In addition to her sports advocacy work, she was also involved in the French suffragette movement and worked to promote women's rights in the workplace and in politics, particularly the right to vote.

Sadly, cancer took Alice from this world in 1957. The next time we see a woman carrying the torch at the Olympics, we ought to be reminded of the incredible achievements of this one-of-a-kind woman. Without her continuous support for women's athletics and her eagerness to seek equality between men and women, the world today and the world of future generations of girls and women in sports would surely be very bleak.

But her fight remains as relevant as ever, with disparity still present in areas of professional sports between men and women. It is up to us to continue her legacy.

Roberta Gibb and Katherine Switzer: Rebel Run

Bobbi's full name is Roberta Louise Gibb. She was born on November 2, 1942, in Cambridge, Massachusetts. The suburbs of this city were the background in which she grew up. Her father was a chemistry professor at Tufts University.

Ever since she was a child and could stand on two legs, she remembers running and loving to do so. The distance through the forest from home to school and back served as a track for her and her friends. But despite it being almost universal that children slow down when they enter their teen years, she did not. The dogs from the neighborhood would keep her company.

Her other passion was sculpture, which made her decide to attend the Boston Museum of Fine Arts and the Tufts University School of Special Studies. Later in life, she produced several pieces dedicated to running; they represent the joy of crossing the finish line as a young woman, a feeling she is most familiar with.

At the age of 20, she met a man who seemed to be designed for her—a middle-distance runner and her classmate at Tufts.

His name was William Bingay. They got married on February 5, 1966.

The first time Bobbi ever witnessed the Boston Marathon was in 1964. Her father had accompanied her, and it was the first time she had ever seen other people running. At the time, the marathon was for men only, but she did not see men running in front of her; she only saw people. The bodies in motion connected with her on a deeper level, bringing to mind the enduring connection between the first humans who stood up on their feet in Africa and the humans running that marathon. It was love. She started training immediately after that life-changing race.

While living in California, once she felt ready to take part, she wrote to the Boston Athletic Association to apply for the 1966 edition of the marathon. Will Cloney, who was the Race director at the time, replied by writing that women were not physiologically able to run the 26 miles of the race. They did not want to take the medical risk. Even decades after Alice's fight, the medical misconception about women's bodies' lack of endurance was still widespread worldwide. Bureaucratically, there was another obstacle; women were not allowed to compete in races longer than a mile and a half. Bobbi could not find that more amusing, given that she was running 40 miles every day. That was the moment she realized her participation in the race was not only for her but for all other women being held back by false beliefs. It had the weight of a political statement.

She took the bus to Boston and arrived a day before the race. Her parents, at first, thought she had gone mad when she told them her plans. But then Bobbi's mother understood her reasons for doing so and offered to drive her to the start line. She was in awe of her mother's finally taking her side. They hugged, and her mother wished her good luck.

Her plan was to pass as a young man. To do so, she dressed in her brother's shorts, her bathing suit, and a blue-hooded sweatshirt to cover her head so competitors around her could not tell she was a girl. She hid among some bushes near the start line until the starting gun went off and jumped in when a group of runners passed right in front of her. At first, nobody noticed something odd about that competitor, but as the minutes went by, the men behind her began to realize she was, in fact, a woman, so she gave in and smiled around. To Bobbi's utter surprise, their reaction was not to demand she leave the race but instead to throw comments at her about their regrets for their girlfriends and wives not running as she did. Even more, they offered to protect her if the race organizers found her and asked her to leave before she could finish.

But the rumors at the sides of the track ran fast, and the press picked them up. Knowing they had something big, the local radio station set up to broadcast her progress, which made the women in the crowd begin looking for her. All those women students at the nearby college wanted to cheer for Bobbi.

When she finally reached the finish line, everyone screeched and cheered, and the Governor of Massachusetts approached and shook her hand. She completed the race in 3:21:40, coming up in the fastest third of the pack. Nevertheless, she was forbidden from attending the post-race dinner.

The front pages of the journals the next day were all dedicated to her. But not everyone was happy with her deed. Director Cloney put into question the participation of Bobbi, even going so far as to doubt that she had run the entire distance. As if it were a Twitter quarrel, she answered by telling him to ask the other male runners, and if he still did not believe her, that was his problem.

As it could not have been otherwise, in the following edition, Bobbi was there to run again. And she remained there for the next four years—the time it took her to get a Bachelor's degree from the University of California. She was denied admission to medical school despite having fulfilled all requirements. The denial made her decide to take another path completely, entering the New England School of Law and receiving her degree four years later, in 1978. While she was working in the Massachusetts State Legislature, she raised her family.

Much time passed, but finally, Bobbi was given the honor of having a statue of herself as the first woman to finish the marathon at the Hopkinton Center for the Arts. She crafted the statue with her own hands—a double honor, no doubt.

The story of Bobbi meets the story of another outstanding woman, precisely at the Boston Marathon.

Kathrine Virginia Switzer was born on January 5, 1947. Her birth coincided with her family's stay in Amberg, Germany, as her father was a major in the United States Army. It was after the end of the Second World War and the Allied occupation of Germany. They returned to the U.S. in 1949.

She started running at the age of twelve with a goal in mind: To join the field hockey team at George C. Marshall High School in Virginia, where she attended. To do so, her father advised her to train and run a mile a day. Hard work would later pay off, as she was selected to join the team. But not only that, she described the trajectory of her evolution during this training as going from a "skinny little insecure kid" to a young, empowered girl.

After graduating from high school, she went on to study at Lynchburg College, a liberal arts school. But two years later, she decided to transfer to Syracuse University. Her desire had shifted toward English literature and journalism.

When Katherine arrived at the new University, she met Arnie Briggs. He was an assistant coach for the men's cross-country team. With permission from the authorities, she began training with the men. A little later, she was telling Arnie that she wanted to run the Boston Marathon. And just like Bobbi, Katherine received the same answer, that women could not possibly run that distance. The medical myths were old and everywhere. But she did not give up, to which he proposed a challenge: If she showed him that she could run the 26 miles, he would take her to the race. Their top mark was 31 miles.

Arnie kept his word and helped her sign for the 1967 race. The rules did not clearly state that women could not run, so she signed with her initials and paid the two required dollars. Of course, the Boston officials thought the name in the entry form belonged to a man when they received it and gave Katherine the number 261.

After much impatience, the day of the marathon arrived. The weather could not have been worse; it was snowing, and the wind was very strong. Katherine was wearing shorts and a top but would not take off her warm-up suit. A decision that helped her pass as a man at the start line. While she felt uneasy, Arnie was untroubled and assured her there would be no problem. Even if there was a problem, Bobbi was running the race as well.

When the gun went off, the pack started moving. During the first mile, all went well until the press noticed her. She waved happily at them. But there was a major difference between Bobbi and her; Katherine had a number on her back. At one point, she started hearing leather shoes running behind her. A mad-looking man grabbed her by the shoulders and tried to rip off her bib number quite violently while shouting for her to leave the race. It was John "Jock" Semple, an important official in the race organization and former runner. She was scared to her bones. When Arnie tried to prevent him from attacking Katherine, he knocked him out of the way. Fortunately, Katherine's soon-to-be husband, Tom Miller, came to their aid and threw the official out to the side of the street.

They continued, but the anger had taken a toll on her. Despite the episode, she said to Arnie that she would finish the race even if she had to do it on her hands and knees. Sadly, the change in beliefs about women's capability for endurance sports depended on it.

Katherine crossed the finish line about an hour after Bobbi. The sense of achievement was other-worldly for her. She knew at that moment she had to continue her fight for women to be allowed to run in official competitions. Sometimes actions produce the spiraling opposite result from what was originally planned.

But people were angry at her audacity. So much so that the Amateur Athletic Union (AAU) changed its rules to explicitly bar all women from participating in races across the country. After some years of trying, Katherine and other fellow runners managed to convince the Boston Athletic Association (BAA) to set up a women's race in 1972. It was not an all-inclusive solution, but at least they could legally participate.

Her life continued, and that same year, she got her master's degree. A little later, she filed for divorce and subsequently married twice—to public relations executive Philip Schaub and runner and author Roger Robinson, to whom she is still married.

Katherine never stopped running, and in 1974 she was the women's winner of the New York City Marathon. She dedicated her life to running on and off the track, becoming a commentator and writer.

Maybe the most curious detail remains that she would later become John Semple's close friend after he changed his mind about women's sports. Everybody has a chance at redemption.

SUPPORT IN THE STRATEGY TO BUILD RESILIENCE

One facet of the concept of support is allowing yourself to get support. We often try to be superheroes, reassuring people around us, or we fail to voice our concerns and try to figure it out all by ourselves. But the key change is asking the universe for support. Once we ask out loud, support will appear for us in some form or shape.

We need support from somebody who believes in us when it is hard to believe in ourselves. Acknowledging and allowing it helps create a structure of support around us. It is a wise decision to create that structure before a feeling of uneasiness or distress arises and before a feeling of "dis-ease" becomes a disease. This internalized uneasiness can lead to concerning symptoms of poor health and chronic illness. Sometimes, it is the fear of showing our vulnerabilities that prevents us from connecting with others for support. It takes courage.

This support structure is more apparent in sports, where it is common to have coaches and trainers, physios, and nutritionists to enable the athlete to perform at their highest potential. And let us not forget the already discussed fans.

The same structure can be applied to us and our day-to-day lives. It can be any kind of support, a dear friend, a family member, a pet that helps us regulate our mental health, or a mentor and life coach who can help us through difficult times. Or all of them.

Other times, in the absence of any external support, we can rely on the universe's power, especially when our dreams and goals are bigger than the life that we know. Deep inside us, there is a fraction of our soul that is connected with this higher power. We can tap into the infinite spirit of life for much-needed support.

But enough about receiving support. Giving support is the other equally important facet of this concept, and one could say it is even more important. The cycle of support starts with giving, not receiving. And if we all take part in giving support to others, we will also receive support and be more receptive to the help offered to us. In science, research has proven that supporting others and volunteering has great benefits for mental and physical health, life satisfaction, social well-being, and depression (Yeung et al., 2018).

Reading the stories of Alice, Bobbi, and Katherine, some of

the points that stand out are precisely the networks of support these women were able to build. They relied on their inner sense of support to aid in the most difficult situations.

Alice had the vision to change sports for women. Sports were her passion, but it was also her belief that equality could be implemented in sports. She drew strength from within herself and the network of people who believed that progress was achievable. She formed the networks and leaned on them when it was necessary. And it would not be a change solely for her own good either; it would be for every woman who had the same passion for sports as she did. She gave and received support.

For Bobbi, support came in the form of Bobbi's mother and the men running that first marathon with her. If we think about it, would the outcome have been the same if, instead of these men having encouraged her to keep on running, they had started treating her badly? We cannot say, but it is something worth reflecting on.

Katherine had Arnie Briggs and her boyfriend Tom at the moment she needed support the most. But the inner force she showed came from the thought of other women running that marathon in the future, just like she was doing at that moment. That was the universe giving her the power she required to cross the finish line.

Small Exercise to Define Your Structure of Support and Grow Resilience

- When was the last time you put in the extra mile to support somebody else who found themselves in self-doubt or a stressful situation? What was your response when somebody asked for your support? And be honest, what did you really think? With what mindset did you help them? Did you perhaps have a feeling of annoyance because it might not have been convenient with your schedule? Or were you able to act truly out of your heart?

- Think about this: With whom could you build a support structure? A strong scaffolding to support your growth and the other person's growth? Write down at least three people and contact them today to talk about the group of "partners in believing" you are setting up.
- To start the cycle of giving and receiving, you could consider a charity donation. Perhaps you can donate some items you no longer need or offer to support a project financially. You can think even bigger and volunteer for a cause of your interest or run a fundraiser at your workplace. There are plenty of ways to start the process; just choose one, get started, and notice what is changing inside yourself.
- And to end this chapter, I would like to share a quote attributed to John Wesley that, in fact, he did not say or write (Watson, 2013), but that is most pertinent nonetheless, and ask you to reflect upon it:

Do all the good you can,
By all the means you can,
In all the ways you can,
In all the places you can,
At all the times you can,
To all the people you can,
As long as you can.

TUNING OUR HONESTY

Honesty and transparency make you vulnerable. Be honest and transparent anyway. –Mother Teresa

INTRODUCTION

S ome cultures consider saying "no" too strong a word, a source of guilt, unkindness, or sometimes disrespect. Maybe it is to avoid disappointment from someone dear. Their entire social interactions and languages are built to say no but, at the same time, avoid directly saying it. Subjects need to figure out what the other person is saying without actually saying it. It can be inferred that this opens up countless possibilities for misunderstanding. For cultures not used to this, it can come across as pointless or even irritating.

Honesty is praised in other cultures—to the point of brutality, some might say. What is undeniable is that dishonesty exists in every culture. Whatever the reason for the lack of honesty and linking the topic in this chapter with the previous, giving and receiving support in the form of *constructive* criticism is our main goal.

This chapter will tell the stories of women in law and politics —two of the most disregarded fields when it comes to honesty —who dared to be honest despite the consequences.

What Does It Mean to Be Honest?

Some ground definitions first.

According to our dictionary of choice (Merriam-Webster), honesty:

1. "Adherence to the facts: sincerity."
2. "Fairness and straightforwardness of conduct."

To the APA Dictionary of Psychology, honesty:

1. "In general, truthfulness, uprightness, and integrity."
2. "In psychotherapy, the ability of an individual to express true feelings and communicate immediate experiences, including conflicting, ambivalent, or guilt-ridden attitudes."

But none of these definitions makes a distinction between being honest to ourselves and/or being honest to others. For short, let us define self-honesty as staying true to our values and needs, acknowledging and accepting our own thoughts, emotions, actions, strengths, vulnerabilities, and areas for growth. It involves questioning our beliefs, biases, and assumptions and being open to discovering uncomfortable truths about ourselves.

Here we have a question: Whose values? As we learned in previous chapters, those values can be personal or cultural.

It is assumed that lies can only be told to someone else. If we think about it for a little bit, we will surely find a moment in our lives when we told lies to ourselves, trying to convince our own minds of something that was not true. Or moments when we actively sought to ignore the truths all of our senses were telling us because of the possible impact they might have.

If we analyze the reasons behind the lies we tell others, we might find good or bad intentions, but when we tell lies to ourselves, do we have bad intentions? Do we want to harm ourselves? Probably not. It is likely to avoid harm or pain. Even strain. If we choose to lie to ourselves, it is not because we do not agree with our personal values; it is because our personal values and needs do not align with cultural values.

Now we can all agree that it is possible and sometimes unavoidable to tell lies to ourselves. We can even agree that it is in the name of survival and comfort. But that state has a short shelf life. You can have a life of fulfilled checklists, but you will never reach true fulfillment if you do not practice honesty with yourself as well.

WOMEN WHO SHAPED HISTORY BY BEING HONEST

Margaret Thatcher: Honesty at All Costs

The Iron Lady: It is hard to escape such a polarizing character. Margaret Hilda Roberts was born on October 13, 1925, in Grantham, England. Her family was very conservative and followed the Christian Methodist Church. Luxury, or even basic services like hot water or an indoor bathroom, were unknown to the young Margaret.

Her father's name was Alfred Roberts, a grocer and preacher. Her mother was Beatrice Ethel Stephenson. Early on, she was immersed in the world of politics because of her father's activities, who was elected mayor of their town.

At 18, she entered Oxford University to study chemistry. One of her mentors was Nobel Prize winner Dorothy Hodgkin. In 1946, she became president of the Oxford University Conservative Association, where she was already speaking against welfare policies being implemented by the current Labour government. A year later, she graduated and went on to work as a research chemist. During her formative years, people around her got to know her slightly unapproachable ways.

Despite her formal education, the political urge was still there somewhere, and, lo and behold, in 1950, she ran for a parliamentary seat at Dartford. She failed to be elected but left a strong impression on her constituents.

Dennis Thatcher, a divorced businessman ten years older than Margaret, offered to drive her to the train station one night after a Conservative Party dinner. That was the start of their relationship. Two years later, they were married. The two complemented each other; he was supportive of Margaret's political ambitions, and she let him do his own thing.

After her marriage, she gave birth to the couple's twins in 1953. On a colorful note, Dennis spent the day of his children's birth playing cricket instead of standing by his wife's hospital bed. At the same time, she dedicated herself to bringing up her family; she studied law and practiced as a barrister.

For a few years, she kept away from politics, but by 1959, she was back into political life and elected as a member of parliament (MP) for the seat of Finchley in the House of Commons. Some time later, she was directly appointed Under-secretary for Pensions and National Insurance.

By 1964, the Conservative Party had lost the election, which gave her time to expand her connections and political views by taking a tour across the United States. At the same time, she was part of the shadow cabinet and later promoted to Education Minister.

The Conservatives were back in power in 1970, and Margaret took the position of Secretary of State for Education and Science. Her inclination toward somewhat heartless austerity would begin to show during this period; she ordered a number of budget cuts that caused a stir. One in particular, a free school milk program cut, earned her the nickname "Thatcher, milk snatcher."

A critique she received often was about her lack of appreciation for her fellow women politicians. Even going as far as to say she did not think a woman would get to enter 10 Downing Street in her lifetime.

But her party would only get one period before being voted out again. At the time, Margaret and the head of the party—Ted Heath—disliked each other intensely. Uncommon as it was at that time, she challenged Ted for leadership. Everybody, from the press to the party's members, thought she had gone mad. And while the Labour Party ruled, she became the leader of the Conservatives on February 11, 1975. She was the first woman to ever hold that position.

Due to her hard speeches and even harder stances against communism, she earned her second and definitive nickname: The Iron Lady. A Russian newspaper did the favor. With the Cold War still going strong, neoliberalism was becoming the norm. Unemployment surged, and labor unions' clashes with the government saw a rise.

On May 3, 1979, the UK had another political swing, and the Conservatives won, with Margaret elected as the first female Prime Minister. True to her beliefs, when she took office, she imposed a series of economic policies intended to control the recession: She cut social spending, raised interest rates, and privatized key industries.

But her most controversial stances were against unions and immigrants. Her name, along with Ronald Reagan's, was associated with absolute deregulation and privatization during this period—and after—a stance that would make her approval ratings fluctuate during her time in office. The result was the financialization of Britain's economy, creating the well-known City of London. But the changes would not be merely economic.

Culturally, the most absolute individualism was fomented. The epitome of her idiosyncrasies is an infamous interview in Women's Own in 1987, where she proclaimed, "They are casting their problems at society. And, you know, there's no such thing as society. There are individual men and women, and there are families" (The Guardian, 2018).

In 1982, Margaret faced a different challenge than the domestic ones she had been going through. On April 2nd, Argentina—at the time ruled by a bloody dictatorship—invaded the Falkland Islands, an archipelago located almost 500 kilometers east of the south coast of the country, to regain its control. A war broke out that lasted a few months, with the UK ultimately winning the war. A win that helped her gain popularity again and thus be elected for a second term in 1983. The sovereignty of the islands remains disputed to this day.

But the term would not be an easy one. The National Union of Miners—the most powerful union in the country—started a long and violent strike over their working conditions and wages. After months of battle, the Union submitted and returned to work. Margaret's government then had free reign to close most of the deep pits.

Disputes over sovereignty were also closer to home. "The troubles," a name given to the civil war taking place in Northern Ireland between the Unionists—protestant citizens who wanted to remain in the United Kingdom—and the Republicans—Catholic citizens who wanted to rejoin Ireland—had been going on for ten years. The conflict had intensified so much that on October 12, 1984, the Irish Republican Army (IRA) set up a bomb at a conference in Brighton. Five people were killed, but Margaret escaped unharmed and became ever more convinced that she had to fight on. But the war grew even bigger and bloodier. It would only be after her leaving the premiership that The Troubles would come to an end. And again, with the question of sovereignty on hold.

The international policies of her government led to the development of a close relationship with Soviet leader Mikhail Gorbachev. A sad episode was when she opposed sanctions against apartheid South Africa, calling Nelson Mandela "a terrorist." A stain that is hard to wash away.

She was voted for a third term in 1987. During this period, she introduced new taxes that made her lose the support of the public and the party. One decisive factor in her downfall was her anti-European orientation. In November 1990, with riots breaking out everywhere and people refusing to pay, her leadership was challenged in the same way she had before, and the party members voted for her to leave office. John Major replaced her as Prime Minister while she returned to her MP position. She retired two years later but was appointed to the House of Lords.

Besides her political career, she also wrote several books and toured as a public speaker after her retirement and until 2000, when she began to show signs of dementia. Dennis passed away in 2003. The disease eventually took away her mobility and voice. She died on April 8, 2013, with parts of her country mourning while others clinked their glasses.

Ruth Bader-Ginsburg: Notoriously Lawful

A woman of the law with a nickname as well: Notorious R.B.G. Joan Ruth Bader was born on March 15, 1933, in Brooklyn, New York. Her parents—Celia and Nathan—were both from working-class Jewish immigrant families from Eastern Europe, with her father as a first generation and her mother as a second. Tragically, her older sister Marylin passed away at six years old from meningitis when Ruth was only a baby. Neither Celia nor Nathan was able to attend college, but a distinctive habit that made Ruth develop a need for knowledge was her mother's taking her to the public library to read books to her. An action that could have been innocent but made a great difference in her development as a child.

As a little girl, she shared her first name with many other girls in her class, so her mother suggested she use her middle name. Besides the law, this little girl developed a passion for opera very early in life when her aunt took her to a performance at a high school near their home. The performance was a special one designed for children to approach the world of opera. It changed her life.

In her teen years, Ruth was already passionate about the realities of her surroundings. That drive led her to work as an editor for the high school newspaper, and her outgoing personality led her to participate in the pep squad. She even graduated early at the age of 15, a day that must have been hard for Ruth as her mother had died the previous day from cancer after a long battle. The family was left helpless, and thus, it was decided that only her brother would be sent to college. The decision made her wait a few years to attend.

She entered Cornell University to study government. There, she met another student, Martin David Ginsburg, a chemistry major who would switch to government not long after. They started a relationship a little while later, and Ruth would say he loved her with her brain. In 1954, after her graduation, they got married and moved to Oklahoma, where Marty had been called to service in the army. Ruth gave birth to a beautiful girl they named Jane a year later.

Ruth's love for the law came to be during a class on constitutional law when her professor made the students focus on the lawyers sitting in the hearing of Joe McCarthy. She became fascinated by the process and thought the law could be a tool to turn the world into a better place. And pay the bills as well.

In 1956, the newbie mother enrolled in Harvard Law School— along with her husband—where the pool of students was over

500 with only nine women in it. She was able to complete her first two years and even became the first female member of the Harvard Law Review. But she was forced to ask for a transfer to Columbia for her third year because Marty had been diagnosed with testicular cancer, and they were not sure whether he would survive the treatment—treatments that were nothing like they are today. It was her first contact with the disease, and it would not be the last one. Infamously, Harvard's dean, Erwin Griswold—the same dean that once asked his female students why they were taking men's spots in law school—denied her the possibility of obtaining her degree from Harvard if she left. So she left and graduated first in her Columbia class in 1959. Much to the happiness of the family, Marty recovered and went back to a normal life.

When she graduated, the task of getting her first job as a lawyer proved to be not just hard but almost impossible. During that period, not a single law firm in New York would offer her a job, even though she had finished first in her class. She had three "disadvantages," as they were regarded at the time: She was a woman, she was Jewish, and she had a four-year-old daughter. It is hard to pinpoint which was the decisive factor. The only position she could aspire to was secretary, and that was in normal circumstances. But she was fortunate enough to have a Columbia teacher advocate for her and compensate for the injustice. She was hired as a law clerk for Judge Edmund L. Palmieri.

Ruth joined the Columbia Law School Project on International Civil Procedure in 1961, a research position that allowed her to travel to Sweden and be in contact with other jurists at Lund University. But most importantly, she was in contact with other forms of society, one where women occupied every space in public life.

After leaving the Project on International Civil Procedure in 1963, she became a teacher of civil procedure at Rutgers Law

School and would teach there until 1972. In the meantime, the couple's second child, James Steven, was born in 1965.

In 1972, the University of Columbia welcomed her as the first tenured professor in the institution's history. That same year, she co-founded the Women's Rights Project at the American Civil Liberties Union (ACLU) and became its chief litigator and director. During her work with the ACLU, she litigated before the Supreme Court some of the most cited cases of discrimination on the basis of gender in the history of the country.

In 1980, President Jimmy Carter nominated Ruth to the U.S. Court of Appeals for the District of Columbia Circuit. At the time, not a single female was seated in a federal court. Therefore, for Ruth to dream of something like that was unheard of. The Senate confirmed her nomination in June of that year. In court, she conducted herself with caution but without fear.

Finally, in 1993, she became a judge of the Supreme Court under the mandate of President Bill Clinton. Her confirmation hearing marked a significant change in the process. She based her strategy on the need for nominees to be judged by their credentials, not their views on possible future subjects. She would not be the only woman; Sandra Day O'Connor was appointed as well. Ruth always credits Sandra for inspiring her, not only as a figure of law but also as a big sister.

One of the stories that testify to the male-dominated world of law was about the black robe judges were required to wear by protocol. It was a piece of formal wear designed for men, as it had an opening to show the shirt and necktie underneath. Sandra and Ruth thought it would be appropriate to add a collar made of lace—called a jabot—to the robe. Later, Ruth would become somewhat of a fashion icon by adding big necklaces and other accessories to her look.

Her stances on the Supreme Court categorized her as a moderate liberal. Worker's rights, women's rights, and separation of church and state were among her natural inclinations. But even though she mainly voted with the liberal bloc, she sometimes strayed from traditional liberal opinions. And she would do so with strong words and gestures. Her colleagues had opinions about her that she took with humor, especially from Antonin Scalia. Although their visions of the law were opposite, their love for opera was shared, a not-so-common taste that would bring them together as friends.

But the importance of her presence there as a woman was to show her male counterparts that sex discrimination existed, something they did not believe. This is a perfect example of why representation is important in every aspect of life.

In 1999, Ruth was diagnosed with colon cancer, for which she underwent surgery. Following the procedure, doctors prescribed chemotherapy and radiation therapy. And although she recovered, in 2009, she was diagnosed again, this time with pancreatic cancer. As the willful woman she was, she beat cancer again and went back to court.

In 2010, Marty died from cancer. The disease seemed to show an especially cruel face to the Ginsburg family. But their 56-year-old marriage was a happy one. One of the most important pieces of advice she ever received was from her mother-in-law. She told her: Sometimes it helps to be a little deaf.

Despite the immense step forward, it was for Ruth to sit on the high bench, she was not free from controversy. During an interview with Katie Couric in 2016 (Ruiz-Grossman, 2021), while promoting her book *My Own Words*, when asked her opinion on Colin Kaepernick's protest, she said it was "really dumb." She later apologized, but in 2021, the same journalist revealed she had edited out even harder remarks. Ruth said athletes like Colin were showing "contempt for a government that has made it possible for their parents and grandparents to live a decent life, which they probably could not have lived in the places they came from."

The especially cruel face of cancer fortuitously showed once again in 2018 when Ruth was hospitalized for a fracture. This time, the nodules were in her lungs. She underwent surgery, and a month and a half later, she was back to work. But the cancer was not over; a few months after her lung surgery, she received radiation therapy for a tumor found again in her pancreas. This time, the tumor would not go away, and on September 18, 2020, she passed away.

Ruth often said that she would keep working as a Supreme Court judge as long as her body and mind let her. And she did. She stayed on the Supreme Court until the day she died. Her nature was not one to step down and *go gentle*.

BEING HONEST AS A WAY TO BUILD RESILIENCE

Whether we agree with Margaret Thatcher's view or not, what comes to mind when we learn of her remarks about Nelson Mandela is the obvious fact that she was brutally honest, both to herself and to others. It might have brought her many problems and setbacks, but she always prioritized her values over what people demanded of her. We can even say that she was a visionary in regard to her anti-Europe stance, taking into account how the Brexit vote would turn out decades later.

Margaret was consistent with her values throughout her life, and it is undeniable that it brought her prestige and respect. As a politician, being consistent and honest are two of the most desired yet elusive traits, which is a tragedy. What we should not even be demanding, as it should be a baseline characteristic of a leader, we are praising. This only causes mistrust in organizations and institutions, so in order to regain trust in them, we need to exercise honesty from the bottom to the top. Start ourselves, and other people will follow. One by one, the individual becomes the group. Just like emotions are contagious, so is honesty. Here, we can clearly see another circle of giving and receiving.

Ruth was somewhat similar. She definitely faced backlash for her controversial remarks, but she apologized. What we can learn from her actions, regardless of whether we choose to accept that apology as sincere or not, is that honesty involves acknowledging our own mistakes. This might be the hardest part of the journey toward an honest life, but it is the most fundamental of the principles to live in harmony with the people around us and ourselves.

The first step in the path to resilience might be honesty, and honesty is about sharing our vulnerabilities. As an example, the first principle of Alcoholics Anonymous (AA) is the principle of honesty, which is considered the first step to recovery. Lack of honesty is a key factor that keeps a person in a vicious cycle—in this case, a cycle of addiction. Being honest is not only about saying the truth; it is more so about practicing the principle of honesty by acting on what we say.

This strategy intertwines with courage as well; one needs to be courageous first and be honest later. Whether it is to face backlash or to put one's public image—with politicians particularly—in question.

Most leaders then avoid honesty in order not to offend anyone. But who told you that it was your right to go through life without ever feeling offended? It is an indivisible part of the human experience. Telling people only what they want to hear is not in their best interest. What is in their—and our—best interests is clarity. As Professor Brené Brown puts it, "Clear is kind. Unclear is unkind" (2018).

In our relationships with others, intentions are everything. Honesty stripped out of empathy is cruelty. Truths are often hard to listen to, and we always have to take into account the context and consequences of telling them. And we can link this aspect of honesty to our previous strategy of support; what better support than having people who love us tell us the truths we refuse to see or are unable to see with the best of intentions? Everything in life is about perspective.

Giving and receiving support means, first and foremost, having the courage to tell our loved ones the truth, which is hard to listen to but will help in the future. And expect no less than the same in return.

Honesty shows a neurophysiological difference in brain activation levels; dishonesty contributes to an increase in activity in specific brain areas, similar to a stress reaction. It all comes back to us.

It also has a positive impact on our mental health: Honest and compassionate communication promotes openness and trust in relationships; it is fundamental for functioning and enduring social and intimate relationships. Honesty promotes trust, prevents harm, and leads to a sense of safety, which allows the individual, community, or society to develop and flourish.

In the last few years, the other side of the research (Levine & Munguia Gomez, 2020) has suggested that people often use honesty when it serves their interests and willingly avoid information about the harm they might have caused. You might be very honest, but if that honesty comes with a *knife* behind it, it is not a virtue and can clash with other important moral values.

Honesty is not a value in itself but rather a tool to do good. Use it wisely.

Small Exercise to Practice Honesty and Grow Resilience

Practicing the characteristics of an honest person:

- Try to see the world through other people's eyes: Understanding that everyone has a story and that it is not our job to judge how these stories started or ended is a sign of empathy. And when telling our stories, exaggerating leads to dishonesty.

- Gossiping or talking behind another person's back jeopardizes relationships. That includes sharing information or secrets that are not ours to share. Honest and direct communication is the only way to maintain healthy relationships. This is showing up as ourselves; putting on a façade only brings unhappiness. It is about embracing all our quirkiness as a part of ourselves because it is what makes us unique.
- When things go wrong, it is wise to be accountable and not blame others or circumstances. Admitting that we have been wrong is part of being human, growing, and learning. Taking responsibility for our actions and learning from them will help us move forward, making sure it does not happen again.
- Matching our words and actions by keeping promises creates trust.
- In stressful situations, keeping a clear mind and an open heart helps us control our emotions and avoid acting on anger.
- Holding grudges, especially against ourselves, is like trying to hurt somebody by throwing hot coals at them; the only person who gets burned is us.
- Our ethics and morals are our values, and compromising them just to keep somebody happy or to fit in a box created by someone else is dishonesty. Even if it is not popular, standing up for what we believe in is a duty to ourselves.
- Let's be honest because it is the right thing to do. "Management is doing things right, leadership is doing the right things" (Drucker, 1954).

8

INSTRUMENTALIZING OUR FAILURES AND SETBACKS

It is impossible to live without failing at something unless you live so cautiously that you might as well not have lived at all, in which case you have failed by default. –J.K. Rowling

INTRODUCTION

F ailure is an indivisible part of success and happiness. Even the classic hero's journey has a moment in which our *extremely talented* protagonist—*the one*—goes through a difficult time. My question is: Would it still be a story worth reading or watching if the characters did not need to overcome themselves? How can a life worth living be static or monotonous? The biggest lessons come from the obstacles on our paths, and we would never know what happiness is without knowing what suffering is as well.

The chosen woman for this chapter is one who changed the face of science and faced countless setbacks and some tragedies herself but was able to overcome them.

Failure and Setback: Definitions

Merriam-Webster: Failure

- "Lack of success."
- "A falling short: deficiency."
- "One that has failed."

And setback is defined:

- "A checking of progress".
- "Defeat, reverse."

None of these definitions are exhaustive, though. So some people might define failure as a lack of success, but it is actually what happens on the way to success. And most importantly, it is contextual. Here is where we need to tie it up to the chapter on values; failure exists in the context of a value system, and in particular, from the perspective of an observer.

The signifier *failure* has changed its signified over the course of centuries; it went from referring to an event in the life of a person to a personal trait. From "you *experienced* a failure" to "you *are* a failure." This has had enormous consequences for the lives of people and changed the value system. As we can infer, knowing a failure is just a temporary event keeps hopes up for the person experiencing the bad moment, but if the failure is somewhat perceived as *part of our DNA,* hope is hard to find.

A WOMAN WHO DIED PURSUING HER DREAM BUT LEFT A LEGACY

Marie Curie: Science as Oxygen

Maria Salomea Skłodowska was born in Warsaw, Poland, on November 7, 1867, into a family of educators, a factor that would prove determinant to her future achievements. Those were the times of the Russian Empire and Russian-controlled Poland. Polish was forbidden to be spoken, and the country's history was not studied.

As it was the reproductive norm at the time, she was the youngest of many children—five, to be precise. They lovingly called the little girl Manya. Her parents—Vladislav and Bronislawa—were high school teachers, one dedicated to physics and mathematics and the other to a position as the director of a private school exclusively for girls.

In those years, the family was going through financial struggles due to poor investments. This situation led to them having to move into the school where Bronislawa worked. When they finally got their own place, Manya was five years old.

Bronislawa suffered from tuberculosis, a situation that would force her to distance herself from the children out of fear of passing the disease to them. She would not hug them or show any kind of physical affection. Protection came first.

At the age of six, Manya started school. Being the youngest, she surprised the adults and the older students when she soon became an over-achiever. Her prodigious memory was both a blessing and a curse for the girl; her parents would make her recite poetry to visitors, which she did not enjoy at all.

Two years later, her older sister Zofia got sick with Typhus and passed away. And two years after the death of Zofia, her mother also died from complications from tuberculosis. These were incredibly hard times for Manya.

Nevertheless, she was driven, and as early as 1883, she had obtained her high school diploma. She finished first in her class in every possible subject. But despite the good performance she showed in her studies, the effort had taken a toll on her; she would suffer from what we now colloquially call "burnout." She spent a year recovering outside the city.

Upon her return, Manya desired to further her education, but the University of Warsaw accepted only men. The University of Paris appeared to be a good substitute, but to raise enough money to study, she and her sister Bronya had to make the decision to take turns attending and working to support each other. Bronya left for Paris first, and Manya stayed to work for a wealthy family as a governess.

The first half of the six years she spent as a tutor would be with the Zorawski family, a family living outside of Warsaw. Among her side activities, she taught local children to read and write, something illegal back then.

During this period, she heard about a secret "Floating University" where people studied science and other subjects. They would get together every time in different places, and women were accepted. It seemed like a good enough but momentary solution. She continued to study alone and would use every resource available to broaden her mind, even to the detriment of her health.

Some months after arriving at the Zorawski family home, Manya met their oldest son, Kamizierz, who was back from University. The dashing young man caught Manya's eye, and the feeling was reciprocated. To the sadness of the couple, his family did not agree to the marriage; she was only a poor governess and "unworthy" of their son. They separated, but Manya kept working for the Zorawskis as her sister depended on her.

By 1889, Manya had returned to Warsaw and begun working for another family. Three years later, she had saved enough to join her sister and new husband in Paris. She lived in a small and lacking attic close to the University. With the little spending money she earned working at the library, she could scarcely eat and pay for the lessons. But she rejoiced in doing what she loved despite the double difficulty the language posed. In 1893, she got her master's degree in physics as the top scorer and continued to study for a second degree in mathematics with a well-earned scholarship.

Two years later, Marie met Physicist Pierre Curie while looking for a laboratory for her research. He was quite a character—still living with his parents at 34, an introvert who felt unease around women but actually thought she was an exceptional woman. The two fell in love and got married on July 26, 1895. The following year, Marie gave birth to their first child, Irene.

She kept on studying while being a mother and earned a doctorate in physics. The subject came from the discovery of the reason a mineral called pitchblende emitted certain kinds of rays. This particular mineral contained uranium or thorium. But after conducting some experiments, the rocks she analyzed emitted more radiation than was previously thought, so what was causing it? The answer was polonium—she named it after her dear country—a non-discovered element, as she announced in 1898. A few months later, she announced the discovery of another radioactive—a term she coined herself—element, radium.

But to prove the discovery, Marie and Pierre—who was now entirely dedicated to his wife's research—had to purify the element. They came close after three years of work and enormous amounts of processed pitchblende. In 1903, Marie was the first woman in Europe to receive a doctorate in science and the first woman to win a Nobel Prize in Physics, shared with Pierre and Physicist Henri Becquerel, for their work on radioactivity. The money that came with it was useful; the fame, not so much.

But as great as their discoveries were, so were the negative consequences they had to face. Radiation exposure and its terrible health effects were not known or studied then. They began showing signs of deterioration; weight loss, pain, exhaustion, and burns in their hands were among the many symptoms.

On December 6, 1904, Marie gave birth to the couple's second child, a daughter they named Eve. The situation seemed to improve when Pierre was appointed professor at the Sorbonne and Marie was appointed chief laboratory assistant.

In 1906, with their lives at a happy peak, tragedy struck when Pierre suffered an accident with a horse-drawn wagon and was killed instantly. Devastated by the loss of her husband and research partner, Marie accepted the position at the University that her late husband had occupied until then. She was the first woman to become a professor at the Sorbonne.

For the next five years, she dedicated all her efforts to the isolation of the two elements she had discovered after some colleagues raised valid questions about inexplicable helium gas emissions. Pure radium was then found to be a solid white metal in normal conditions. For her work, she was awarded a second Nobel Prize in 1911, this time in chemistry. She was the first person to do so.

When the First World War broke out, Marie helped by lending her expertise to the medical teams. She taught the personnel how to use X-ray equipment to find shrapnel and bullets in the wounds of convalescent soldiers.

After the war, she became director of the Paris Radium Institute, and one failed attempt and four years later, she was elected to the French Academy of Medicine. By this time, Marie's health had deteriorated to the point where her sight and hearing were very limited. To treat her cataracts, she underwent several eye surgeries. Scientists were finally becoming aware of the immense negative effects radiation had on living creatures. But for Marie, it was too late. She spent her last years torn between overseeing the work in the labs and traveling to raise funds for further research. Not a soul would keep her away from her labs as long as she could move around.

This legendary woman passed away on July 4, 1934, from aplastic anemia caused by her prolonged exposure to radiation.

Her legacy lived on in her daughter Irene—a Nobel Prize In Chemistry winner as well—and in present times through her groundbreaking scientific discoveries and the countless women she inspired to do science.

THE STRATEGY OF TURNING CRISIS INTO OPPORTUNITY

Owning Our Vulnerability

Failures belong to our journey of growth. And expanding on a definition, failure is not the opposite of success; it is a part of success. Failures and setbacks are there to help us understand what did not work along the way. It is not there to define us or hold us back in our journey.

We look at failures with a certain mindset and decide if they have a positive or negative outcome. The problem lies in the common societal understanding of dichotomies: We mainly think in terms of black or white, win or lose, good or bad, or body or mind. We have the tendency to categorize everything to give some order to the information we store in our minds.

As hinted at before, the common understanding of a setback or failure as something bad is often associated with shame. The heavy feeling of not being good enough or unworthy and the associated fear of not being deserving of love anymore, pushes us on a path of disconnection and abandonment as social beings.

These heavy feelings bring intense emotional pain when the experiences we have or our actions result in failure. It might be associated with our upbringing and the way our parents and culture responded to mistakes when we were children. Was there some form of punishment involved? If that is the case, the connotation of mistakes and failure is likely attached to guilt and sometimes even shame.

Brené Brown (2013) distinguishes between guilt and shame, with guilt being a consequence of behavior that goes against our values and societal norms. In fact, guilt can be quite helpful in order to change our behavior if we accept that feelings of psychological discomfort can be equal to guilt.

Whereas, shame is the identification of oneself as *being* bad. She adds that shame is more likely to be the source of destructive, hurtful behavior than a tool to arrive at a solution. She goes on to say that fear of disconnection, grown from profound shame, can make us dangerous. When feeling shame, the most common deflective strategy is anger. And we can see that these behaviors lead to trauma in others, which again causes shame, and the spiral of violence goes on and on.

Research (Graham, n.d.) in the prison population and youth justice system has shown that shame is strongly associated with a lack of self-love, experienced from a young age as rejection and violence. The fear of shame is also the fear of one's inherent unlovability and a fundamental motivation for violence.

In order to overcome shame within ourselves and in the eyes of others, love shown through empathy and compassion is the answer. We will be focusing on the strategy in the next chapter.

Suppose we were able to turn the connotation around and not think of failure as something shameful. If we instead used a loving approach with ourselves, as we would with a child who has made a mistake, we would not experience self-shaming. We would be thinking about failures as something positive, a sign of growth, appreciating the opportunity to learn how to approach problems differently, and acknowledging them as a sign that we are truly on our way. We could finally see the world with different eyes.

Once you are able to get into this mindset, you will be looking for failures. You would almost want failure to make sure you learn everything that is required on your journey. Failures allow you to learn and grow faster and more intensely.

Essentially, there are no failures or setbacks; there are only challenges and opportunities.

As this book centers on building resilience, we must talk about the connection between vulnerability and resilience. In order to build resilience, we must first suffer emotional and/or physical wounds. If we accept vulnerability as the "susceptibility to developing a condition, disorder, or disease when exposed to specific agents or conditions" (American Psychological Association, n.d.) or the capability "of being physically or emotionally wounded" (Merriam-Webster, 2019), then it can be inferred that resilience cannot exist without vulnerability.

Acknowledging and embracing vulnerability is a key component of developing resilience. This way, we are open to understanding our needs and developing effective coping mechanisms to never lose hope for a better future. Flexibility helps us adapt to the setbacks we will surely face and decide, without fear, what is best for us.

Making vulnerability work in our favor is the most important lesson we can take from Marie Curie. Her life was marked by countless setbacks. The passing of her mother and little sister was the first encounter she had with the tragedy of death. Despite this, she continued studying and excelling because it was what her mother had taught her—learning was beautiful. But getting a degree in science was something different. She faced the difficulty of studying science in her own country, the lack of money, and the forbidden institutions for women.

Along with her sister, they acknowledged the problem they were facing and found a solution together that would work for both. They encouraged each other and kept their promises. After years and much patience, Marie had enough money to finally move to Paris, and she used the opportunity to the fullest.

The sudden death of her husband was another one of the tragic setbacks she suffered. But she mourned him by taking over the position of professor he had held. What better way to honor him?

She drew courage from the tragedies and poured it into her passion and vision with the support of her family.

An Invitation to Practice Self-Love, Overcome Internalized Shame, and Look at Failures as Opportunities to Grow Resilience

Empathy and love are the antidotes to shame.

Show yourself some love:

- Write a letter to yourself, but to a much younger version of yourself—a letter filled with empathy, love, and understanding for whatever happened or whatever you might have done wrong or failed to do entirely. Take some time for this and go all in; turn your phone off, and eliminate any other possible distractions. Use language that is forgiving and enabling. Have a box of tissues close at hand for when you knock down the wall of self-defense, and empathy and love kick in.

9

DEPLOYING OUR KINDNESS AND COMPASSION

When we know ourselves to be connected to all others, acting
compassionately is simply the natural thing to do.
—Rachel Naomi Remen

INTRODUCTION

C ompassion and empathy are the glue that holds our social
structures together.

When talking about compassion, we are at risk of falling into
the easy dichotomy between having compassion for humans or
animals. Lately, there have been discourses focused on taking
care of the environment and nature but treating humans as a
plague or the evil of this planet. What these ideas fail to recognize is that we, as humans, are also part of nature. We are not a
separate entity arbitrarily above the rest of the living beings on
this Earth. We *are* animals, whether we like it or not.

The challenge lies in having compassion for everyone and
understanding that all creatures experience some form of
suffering they are trying to overcome. On a spiritual level, we

are all the same and connected. With this thought, it becomes easier to have compassion for all.

The next two women discussed in this chapter acknowledged that and did not make a difference when dispensing love and compassion around.

Defining Compassion

Compassion is defined by Merriam-Webster (2009) as:

- "Sympathetic consciousness of others' distress together with a desire to alleviate it."

The APA Dictionary (n.d.) defines compassion as:

- "A strong feeling of sympathy with another person's feelings of sorrow or distress, usually involving a desire to help or comfort that person."

Kindness in the Merriam-Webster (2019) dictionary:

- "The quality or state of being kind."

And to the APA Dictionary (n.d.) is:

- "Benevolent and helpful action intentionally directed toward another person. Kindness is often considered to be motivated by the desire to help another, not to gain explicit reward or to avoid explicit punishment."

During my school years, I was almost suffocated with Latin and Ancient Greek and studies around ancient cultures. My teacher, who always emphasized the importance of going back to the true source of a text, as he was never satisfied with a translation of the original, had these words for me: "If you can, always drink from the well. Avoid the downstream water. You never know if it might be contaminated." Well, let us see how this might help us find a deeper understanding of the word.

The word compassion is made out of two words: "com" and "passion." *Com* is a Latin word, and *passion* comes from the Greek word *pathein*. *Com* means "together, together with, or combined," and in Latin, it is also used as a prefix to intensify the meaning. *Pathein* means "to suffer" and plays a big role in Greek mythology and Ancient Greek theater to build up a hero's story toward catharsis. (Online Etymology Dictionary, n.d.)

Catharsis is another Ancient Greek word with a deep meaning: "Cleaning the soul." A character who is on a journey of suffering, and throughout the journey, their soul evolves into a new form of being, having gained strength and growth on the way, now ready for the next lesson in life that might include suffering again.

This concept is also anchored in the Buddhist belief systems of Dharma, Reincarnation, and Karma. Many other cultures have this concept deeply embedded in their belief systems as well. A rather simple version of this concept is reflected in the common saying: "No pain, no gain."

The word compassion is often used interchangeably with the word empathy, but they are not the same. While the former refers to a "feeling for another," the latter refers to a "feeling as another." This is a response stemming from compassion, full of warmth and care. Compassion can also be defined as the root of empathy; to achieve a capacity for empathy, we must first feel compassion.

Another aspect worth mentioning is the practical stage of compassion. After the feeling is noticed, action needs to come.

As for the question of compassion being something inherent to the human being or something learned, research (Cook, 2013) has shown that it comes with us into the world. Our capacity to feel what others are suffering is coded within us before we can learn what morality is. Even the concept of punishment and fairness seems to be something we are born with.

With all these concepts, let us meet the women who practiced compassion in ways that had not been displayed before.

A KIND WOMAN WHO CHANGED THE FACE OF BIOLOGY

Jane Goodall: Empathy as a Scientific Tool

This is a woman known for her connections, not just with human beings but primarily with chimpanzees. She was born Valerie Jane Morris-Goodall in Hampstead, London, England, on April 3rd, 1934. Her father was Mortimer Herbert and her mother was Margaret Myfanwe Joseph, an engineer—then turned race car pilot—and a novelist, respectively. Jane was the oldest of two daughters by four years.

Sometimes, seemingly insignificant daily decisions, such as Jane's father buying her a big stuffed chimpanzee during her first year in this world, can amount to life-changing events. Not only for the person directly impacted by this decision but for the people surrounding them as well, and in the case of Jane, even the lives of simians. Jubilee, the stuffed animal in question, scandalized her mother's friends, but contrary to their fears, it is, to this day, still loved and taken care of by Jane.

Like many of the fathers from that time, Mortimer enlisted in the army in 1939, when England declared World War II. He was posted to France and had minimal contact with his family until the end of the war. Sadly, the couple filed for divorce not long after, and given the social stigma a divorce brought to families, the poor but conscious little Jane wrote a letter to her father asking him to wait until her 12th birthday. Her mother was the main pillar for Jane throughout the process.

During childhood, Jane and her sister would spend most of their time at her maternal grandmother's farmhouse. The home was located in Bournemouth on the south coast of England; it was a refuge full of farm animals that housed the women in Jane's family. A place she still owns and visits whenever she needs time alone. There she became fascinated by wild and domestic animals, including her dog Rusty, whom she always credits with having taught her much about animals in her youth.

Jane's first encounter with questions about the fauna and its behavior came when the elders assigned her the task of picking up the eggs. The curious girl was four years old and wondered how the hens could lay eggs when there was no visible hole for them to come out of. To witness the event, she hid in one of the coops and waited four hours until one of the hens finally laid an egg. During all that time, she was nowhere to be found, and her mother, extremely worried, had even called the police. But the moment the excited child came running from the yard with the egg in her hand, Margaret did the only thing that would encourage her daughter: She sat down and listened to her story.

She was an avid reader of adventure stories, which helped her develop the desire to go to Africa. Even though the family had little money and almost none to spend on books, she would save every penny they gave her to buy some from the local secondhand bookstore.

In her youth, she was enrolled at Uplands Private School. Although she was a good student, the routine was utterly dull for someone with her character. The entries in her diary bear testament to this fact. But she could come across as *too much talk* given the fact that she finished with very good grades and even won two prizes for her essays. Her major interests were English, Biology, and History.

At the request of her mother, she enrolled in London's

Queen Secretarial College in 1953 and graduated a year later. After graduation, she took jobs at Oxford and Bournemouth and was an occasional waitress and part-timer at a film company.

Two years later, Clo, a friend of hers from school, invited her to Kenya. But her excitement would have to build up for two more years as she saved money for the trip from England to Kenya. Not long after arriving in Nairobi, she found a job and had the opportunity to meet Louis Leakey, a British paleontologist. He was the curator of the Coryndon Museum of Natural History.

Louis thought Jane would make the perfect candidate to study apes in the wild. He even thought women were more observant than men. According to his theory, following Darwin's, the link between humans and primates was yet to be found, and this region in Africa had the answers. Thus began her career as a researcher. Something virtually impossible today as she had no credentials to conduct such endeavors. Add to this the fact that it would be the first time a study of such characteristics was to be carried out, and by a woman, no less.

Louis hired her as a secretary first and sent her to the Gombe Stream Reserve in Tanzania in 1960. The trip was a hard one, spanning months. The difficulty laid in the access to the site where the chimpanzees lived, a place only reachable by boat through a stream, given the dense rainforest, valleys, and steep hills. Her mother traveled with her for the first few months, as authorities thought a woman alone could not survive in the wild. But for them, the major complication was the civil war that broke out in the Congo, with refugees flocking to Gombe. This made it impossible for the authorities to allow Jane, her mother, and a cook who accompanied them to travel to the stream. They had to wait for several weeks in a prison camp for the situation to calm down.

The day came when Jane finally arrived and looked from the shore at the forest, amazed by the massivity, and it felt unreal, as she recalled later. At first, it was a difficult task; she could not get close to the chimpanzees. Up until that point, researchers were taught to never engage in the social spaces of their subjects of study; they would give them numbers for identification. Jane subverted all this by naming every one of them and fully immersing herself in their habitat, even imitating their habits. With patience and consistency, it took her two years to gain the trust of half the chimpanzees in the reserve. She believed that empathy was the critical factor in detecting changes in humor or attitudes and, therefore, complex social dynamics.

Among the many discoveries Jane made were the facts that primates are not herbivores, use tools, and wage wars between *tribes* for the control of territory. Inside each group, a system of castes functions, with a male at the top. Individuals with distinctive personalities develop long-standing bonds and rituals. Similar to humans, they show complex body language and can learn from their mothers—the task of raising the offspring lays on the females—through observation, imitation, and repetition.

Six months after Jane arrived at Gombe, National Geographic agreed to finance the study—as they were running out of money —and sent photographer and filmmaker Hugo Van Lawick to document her work. The Dutch Baron caught her eye, so much so that they got married in 1964.

The following year, Jane earned a Ph.D. in Ethology at Cambridge University, at Louis's insistence. During her stay in Gombe, the money for research was the main concern for him, and as cautious as he was, he told Jane that he may not always be there to get the money. To do so herself, she needed a degree. That is how she enrolled directly in the Ph.D. Later, she admitted how important the teachings had been to her work.

Hugo's film came out around this time, a release that would bring Jane significant notoriety. Their only child together was born in 1967, a boy named Hugo Eric Louis but lovingly called

Grub by his mother. It was a fulfilling time for Jane, who had a family and could do what she loved, being around and writing about apes. However, Jane and Hugo's marriage was not always easy, and they struggled to balance their careers with their family lives.

In addition to her struggles with marriage and commitment to motherhood, Jane also faced emotional challenges throughout her research. She formed close bonds with many of the chimpanzees in her study group, and she was devastated when they died or were killed by poachers. One of her closest research subjects was a chimpanzee named Flo, whom Jane considered a friend. When Flo died, Jane was inconsolable, and she wrote movingly about her grief in her book *Through a Window*. She has also continued to write and speak about her personal experiences, including her struggles with depression and anxiety, which she has attributed in part to the emotional toll of her work with chimpanzees.

In 1971, she published one of her most popular books, *In The Shadow of Man*, with photographs from Hugo's collection. In an engaging book, she achieved a balanced blend of science and entertainment. It would, of course, not be her last book.

Among her many achievements, she was a professor at Stanford University and was appointed honorary visiting professor of Zoology at The University of Dar es Salaam, located in Tanzania.

Jane and Hugo's marriage lasted a decade, and in 1974, they got divorced on good terms. It would not be her only marriage. The following year, she married Derek Bryceson, a Tanzanian MP and director of National Parks. Tragically, Derek passed away from cancer in 1980. It was very sudden, and for Jane, returning to Gombe was the way to come to terms and heal. She saw the cycle of life in the jungle and learned to put things into perspective.

In 1977, Jane Goodall founded the Jane Goodall Institute, intending to protect and further study the chimpanzees at the

Gombe Reserve. And she had urgent reasons to do so. By the 1980s, chimpanzees had become an endangered species. The rainforests they used to live in were being decimated and their resources taken away. She realized the problem in the struggle between the farmers who needed new land to cultivate—cutting the trees in the park to sell as timber—and the need to preserve the wildlife was poverty. Unless this was addressed first, the solution would never be permanent.

When her book *The Chimpanzees of Gombe* came out, she took the opportunity during a conference at the Chicago Academy of Sciences in 1986 to start a campaign to raise awareness among people about the dangers these creatures faced due to deforestation, bush-meat trade, trafficking, and the use of animals in medicine and beauty research. A few years later, the Institute launched programs—one of which was named Roots & Shoots, a global youth initiative—that focused on education, family planning, water management, sustainable agriculture, and microcredits for women.

Jane and the people at the Institute were successful in stopping deforestation, and now the park has been steadily increasing its green surface for a number of years. Not only this, but she could put pressure on the medical community to reduce animal testing and cross-species organ transplants.

Her advocacy work continued to be recognized throughout her life. She has received numerous honors and awards, including being named a UN Messenger of Peace in 2002. In 2016, a documentary film about her life, *Jane*, was released.

At the age of 88, she remains active and greatly inspires people to pursue dreams of scientific research and adventure well into wet-hot jungles and white desserts. But her main concern is teaching parents to support and encourage the curiosity of children, as her wonderful mother did with her.

Louise Hay: Compassion for the "Undeserving"

Helen Vera Lunney was born on October 8th, 1926, in Los Angeles, California. Her father, Henry John Lunney, divorced her mother, Veronica Chwala, a silent film actress when she was 18 months old. Helen was then sent to a foster home for a short period until her mother took her back in. On her fifth birthday, her mother remarried a man named Ernest Carl Wanzenreid, who would make life hell for both of them.

In the beginning, everything seemed fine. But as time went by, he began to show violent behavior toward them. He was emotionally and physically abusive for the first few years. Not only was she the victim of an abusive stepfather, but she also became the victim of a pedophile neighbor who sexually assaulted her when she was still a child. He was sentenced to 16 years in prison for the crime.

Later, when she entered adolescence, it was her stepfather who started sexually assaulting her. Among these adults, Helen decided she could no longer endure the pain of her situation and left home at the age of 15. She did not have any money, nor did she possess social skills of any kind. And the fact that she was a high school dropout did not help either.

For the first few months, she had sporadic relationships with men who took an interest in her. Within a year, she got pregnant and had a baby. As lost as she felt, the obvious conclusion was that she needed to give up the baby for adoption. Thus, she looked for a family that would adopt and take good care of the child. She found a lovely couple and lived with them for the last two months of her pregnancy. After the birth, Helen and the couple made all the necessary arrangements, and a few days later, she left.

Her utter concern for her mother's well-being would make her go back home. She convinced her to move out of that house with her, and both of them left for good. For a year, Helen took care of her mother, and when she felt Veronica would be alright without her, she left again, this time for Chicago.

For the next five years, she earned a living by working in dime stores and other low-paying jobs. But with a desire to change her monotonous life, she moved again to New York City, where she started working various jobs until she eventually found one as a fashion model. Around this time, she adopted the first name for which she would be internationally recognized: Louise.

By 1954, Louise had met Andrew Hay, an English businessman, and married him. She gave up her modeling career in order to focus on her role as a wife. It was fourteen years of a happy marriage that would end on a sad note for her as Andrew asked for a divorce and left with another woman. Doubt and feelings of failure flooded her head and stayed with her for the next few years.

Desperate to find a way out, she came across the Church of Religious Science. It was there that she found the much-awaited change her life needed. She was eventually drawn to the world of metaphysics and began attending spiritual meetings and classes. For some time, she immersed herself in the study of New Thought and became a licensed practitioner.

In the 1970s, Louise started speaking at the Church of Religious Science in New York City, where she focused on the power of positive affirmations and the connection between mental and physical health. She began conducting workshops and writing books on these topics.

In 1977, Louise was given the test she needed to confirm her belief when she was diagnosed with vaginal cancer. Looking back at her childhood, it seemed like a message. She decided to change her lifestyle to a healthier one, to let go of her resentment, and to forgive everything that had happened to her. Her main goal was to understand her parents and the reasons for their negligence. And she managed to do so. She kept the positive routine for six months, at the end of which doctors could no longer find traces of cancer.

With all the knowledge and personal experience she had collected until then, she published her book *You Can Heal Your Life* in 1984, which explored the connection between emotional and physical health and included a list of common illnesses and their potential emotional causes. This book was included in the best-selling lists and has sold over 50 million copies worldwide.

In those days, the AIDS epidemic was reaching its highest point, and Louise was asked to help by setting up a support group. Prejudice and marginalization were the norms for patients with AIDS, but to her; it was only natural to be there for them—the group was composed mostly of men; they were in need of help. She made the men take a positive approach by letting go of resentment and moving away from the victims' mindset. The first group was composed of six men, but by the end of 1984, there were 90 people crowded into Louise's living room. The group then moved to a much bigger location and was lovingly renamed the "Hay Rides" by the attendees. These people were never treated with disdain or in a condescending manner but with respect and love, which helped make the gatherings a success.

In 1984, Louise founded Hay House, a publishing company focused on self-help and spiritual topics, and the following year, she set up a foundation to financially help people in need.

Louise continued to write and speak on topics related to personal growth and spiritual development until her death on August 30th, 2017. She lives in her teachings and in the minds of the people she helped throughout her life.

COMPASSION AS THE INTENTION BEHIND THE STRATEGY FOR RESILIENCE

Initially, the task of writing a few paragraphs about compassion and how it leads to contribution seemed very easy, but soon some questions arose. I started to wonder if I would be doing these words justice. With my limited knowledge, am I qualified to elaborate on these at all? What do they really mean, and what is the meaning for me?

I once read somewhere—and I cannot recall where—about H.H. Dalai Lama's teacher Ling Rinpoche saying, "I am only a worm in the big universe of spiritual beings." If such a well-educated and spiritual person considers himself "only a worm," how could I feel confident in even trying to grasp these two words?

On a spiritual level, the answer would be to start with what you can, from where you are with what you have, and let the spirit do the rest.

Understanding Compassion

Compassion should not be confused with pity. Pity creates a distance between beings as it lacks togetherness, and even worse, it creates an unnecessary hierarchy between the sufferer and the non-sufferer or observer. It also implies that there is such a thing as a "non-sufferer." But according to Buddhist studies, every being has one thing in common with everybody else, and that is suffering at some stage in life.

So when we feel the need to help—to support—others, we must think carefully about the *how*, as it could put the sufferer in a helpless position, a victim role, and wait for the rescuer. It may not allow the sufferer to go on their personal journey of suffering and find their way toward experiencing catharsis. It takes away the opportunity for growth and spiritual development. H.H. Dalai Lama (Gyatso, 2019) explains that a compassionate attitude needs to go hand in hand with reason and patience. And the key to mastering compassion, reason, and patience is waiting for the challenging situation to present itself and then attempting to put them into practice.

It seems much easier to feel compassionate about our loved ones, but the best teachers helping us develop true compassion are our difficult moments and enemies. They teach us by giving us the opportunity to practice tolerance and develop a peaceful mind. For all of us who cherish compassion and love, being grateful for all the opportunities, including the challenges, is essential.

It can also happen that enemies become friends in a change of circumstances. If we are truly open to practicing compassion, these are the moments that test us. Anger and hatred are harmful forces, and our focus and time should be put into training our minds to reduce their negative effects. "These are the forces we most need to confront and defeat, not the temporary enemies who appear intermittently throughout life" (Gyatso, 2019, pp. 43).

Compassion has a strong notion of togetherness—noticing and acknowledging another being and their suffering. It means getting close to one another, with all the suffering and baggage that comes along, expressing a sense of connectedness, and with that connectedness, providing strength and support. Support in the form of creating a safe space for development and growth and, by doing so, easing the load of suffering. This German proverb captures it well: "A sorrow shared is a sorrow halved" ("*geteiltes Leid is halbes Leid*"). This allows the human being in suffering to experience validation of their being and their values; it creates an atmosphere of equality and respect for both the sufferer and the compassionate being. It allows diversity, new ideas, and both beings to find their purpose. It also allows reflection, introspection, and vulnerability without judgment, which opens up a new connotation: contribution. And once we find our purpose, our task of building resilience becomes clear. As the Buddha says: "True love comes from Understanding."

The spiritual belief that "all is one," that we are all connected with each other through the higher power breathing within us, is reflected in just one word: compassion. It is as if that was the purpose of an individual—to contribute to the greater common good.

As it can be inferred, the concepts of support intertwine with the concepts of this chapter; compassion and empathy are the bases for support, and this can take the form of what I like to call contributions. Contributions are the actions taken when we have found that compassion within us. Compassion leads to contribution, which then leads to altruistic actions, often seen in volunteering. Research (Yeung et al., 2018) has shown that volunteering increases the mental well-being of volunteers by creating a sense of connectedness, belonging, and purpose, which are very important elements within a resilient individual. So let us practice volunteering without limits.

We have addressed compassion for others, but what about self-compassion? Well, the answer is fairly simple. We must treat ourselves with as much compassion as we would someone else. Simple but effective.

In the language of Dr. Kristin Neff (2009) and Buddhist teachings, self-compassion has three main components: Self-kindness versus self-judgment, a sense of common humanity versus isolation, and mindfulness versus overidentification. The first means being understanding of our failures and being kind. The second refers to recognizing the shared human experience of imperfections. The third point points to our awareness of our emotional or personal state without exaggerating or downplaying. I would like to add my take on it, too; self-compassion is the first step toward self-forgiveness and inner healing.

Now, based on science, research (Neff et al., 2007) has

shown that self-compassion is associated with numerous psychological and emotional benefits. It can contribute to increased emotional well-being, reduced self-criticism, improved resilience, greater self-esteem, and enhanced coping with stress. Self-compassion also fosters healthier relationships and promotes a more positive and balanced approach to life. With all these positive points, what is now our excuse to not allow ourselves to be self-compassionate?

Jane's and Louise's Compassion

To Jane, empathy and compassion were not only a way of life but also tools to better do scientific research. It may seem odd for us now—as it did back then—to think about pouring emotion and connection into the hard sciences. But it was precisely this action that allowed her to become one of the top researchers on simians in the world.

The connections with animals and humans alike bring joy, but they also bring pain. We need to be prepared to feel sadness and not shy away from it, as it is part of the human experience. Jane felt that pain when her beloved chimpanzees suffered.

Because what could be the alternative? To isolate from all connection to other living beings, and I ask, is that a life worth living? Profound love and joy can only be felt when we are open to feeling sadness and frustration too.

Louise's journey was a little different. We can clearly see that she went through a difficult time until she found her self-compassion. Cancer was only defeated when she was able to forgive herself and others and move on, getting rid of her resentment and anger.

Compassion, love, and respect for other humans came after she learned to be compassionate to herself. She passed on the *virus* of compassion and helped her community in ways nobody else had been willing to do until then. She taught that every-body deserves love, regardless of who they are.

Small Exercise to Practice Compassion and Grow Resilience

- Use the vision/dream from the previous chapter and reflect on how your dream is compassionate and kind to yourself and others. Think about how it also benefits others.
- Do some "random acts of kindness" to another person throughout your day for the next seven days, and notice how something changes in yourself and around you.
- Observe and notice your self-talk for the next few days. What are you telling yourself? Is it critical or even derogatory? If that is the case, begin by being kind and compassionate to yourself; use words of compassion and approval, like you would encourage and cheer for your best friend. Do this for the next seven days and see what happens.
- And to end this chapter, I would like to share a quote by Martin Luther King Jr.: "Darkness cannot drive out darkness; only light can do that. Hate cannot drive out hate; only love can do that" (1963, p. 47).

10

MAINTAINING OUR PERSISTENCE AND PERSEVERANCE

Persistence is what makes the impossible possible, the possible likely, and the likely definite. –Robert Half

INTRODUCTION

The dotted line that draws the process of building resilience has ups and downs. But what binds the dots together is, without a doubt, persistence, and perseverance; these are the backbone of resilience. These two traits are related but slightly different in concept, and we will see that in the next sections. You will find that the stories of these seemingly alien women have these two traits in common.

Definition of Persistence and Perseverance

Persistence is defined in the most general way (Merriam-Webster, n.d.):

1. "The action or fact of persisting."
2. "The quality or state of being persistent."

According to the New Oxford American Dictionary (1999), persistence:

3. "The fact of continuing in an opinion or course of action in spite of difficulty or opposition."
4. "The continued or prolonged existence of something. The word is derived from the original Latin of the same spelling, meaning "continuing steadfastly.""

If we go into a particular field, namely psychology, which is the field we lean on the most to build this book, Cloninger et al. (1993) describe persistence:

5. "Being persistent is an important character trait in psychology and defines persistence as the tendency to continue an activity despite frustration, fatigue, or dissatisfaction."

And our friends at the APA Dictionary of Psychology (n.d.) define persistence as:

6. "The quality or state of maintaining a course or action or keeping at a task and finishing it despite the obstacles (such as opposition or discouragement) or the effort involved. Also called 'perseverance.'"

Merriam-Webster (2019) defines perseverance as:

- "Continued effort to do or achieve something despite difficulties, failure, or opposition: the action or condition or an instance of persevering: steadfastness."

The APA Dictionary only defines perseverance as persistence.

The root of the word perseverance comes from Latin, with *perseverus* meaning "very strict or earnest," per- (a prefix added to verbs to intensify or multiply their meaning) + *severus* meaning "severe or serious."

It is also known as psychological resilience, a term coined by psychologist Emmy E. Werner in the 1970s.

Now I would like to make an important distinction. There is a significant difference between perseverance and obsession.

Perseverance involves following a course of action or result, fuelled by passion and determination, and pushing through challenges and difficulties because there is a visible destination.

Obsession, on the other hand, is a restless preoccupation with something, and it is seen as irrational or unreasonable when compared to societal norms. Thoughts are dominated by this one idea, and there is an inability to focus on something else.

So, while the first is mainly regarded as a positive character trait, as it depends entirely on will, the second is often perceived as a negative trait, an obstacle in itself, and not necessarily a desire stemming from the will of the individual.

WOMEN WHO PERSISTED AND PUSHED THROUGH THE PATRIARCHY

Rosalind Franklin: A Photograph of Injustice

Rosalind Elsie Franklin was born on July 25th, 1920, in Notting Hill, London, to a wealthy and politically influential Jewish family. Ellis Arthur Franklin—a banker and teacher—and Muriel Frances Waley—who dedicated her life to raising her offspring—were parents to five children, including Rosalind. With a family of three boys and two girls, that home must have been far from a silent one.

Rosalind's interest in the hard sciences probably did not manifest out of thin air; her father taught electricity, magnetism, and history at the Working Men's College. From an early age, she impressed adults with her mathematical skills and excelled in almost every school subject, with one exception: music. But given that her interests laid elsewhere, this did not present a problem. She was educated at St. Paul's Girls' School in London during the last period of her secondary education.

At the age of 18, she entered Newnham College, Cambridge, to study chemistry. With the laboratory being a world-leading center in the subject, her main interest would be focused on X-ray crystallography—a technique that uses X-rays to determine the structure of molecules. During these years, she was already arriving intuitively—as her notebooks show—at some of the most important scientific discoveries in chemistry and biology of the last century. By 1941, she had obtained her degree in chemistry, graduating with honors.

After her graduation, she would set out to work at the physical chemistry laboratory. Although she had been awarded a research fellowship, Ronald George Wreyford Norrish, head of the laboratory, made life impossible for Rosalind; he would not give her meaningful work to do and would often engage in arguments. She utterly despised him. The situation lasted a year, after which she resigned.

In the historical context of the Second World War, Rosalind went on to work as an assistant research officer at the British Coal Utilisation Research Association (BCURA). There, she studied the structure of coal and its changes when subjected to heating. Her discoveries had practical applications; gas masks used in the war were improved thanks to her research. She earned a Ph.D. in physical chemistry for this work from Cambridge University in 1945.

As a little girl, she studied languages, with French among them. This was a factor—as well as some of her dear French friends—for her to decide to move to Paris to continue her work at the *Laboratoire Central des Services Chimiques de l'État* under the supervision of Jacques Mering. Coal and other carbonized materials were still her main topics of research. Using X-ray diffraction, she discovered the differences in the order in which these materials' molecules were organized upon heating.

It is said that Rosalind was quite smitten with Jacques, and he certainly appreciated her for her brain and beauty. The problem was that he was married and even had a mistress.

In 1951, Rosalind returned to London and began working at the biophysics research unit of the Medical Research Council at King's College. The unit was run by John Randall, who chose to have a group of professionals in various fields dedicated to researching the same questions—interdisciplinary cooperation was the key to success, according to him. Sadly, due to misunderstandings at the moment of her arrival with Maurice Wilkins, the deputy director of the unit, and personality clashes between them later, the original plan of John for Maurice, Rosalind, and Ph.D. student Raymond Gosling to work together came crashing down.

Rosalind's personality came across "with an air of superiority" to many of her colleagues, and she certainly had a sharp edge about her. She never fell short in her criticism, especially toward her fellow countrymen, with a sense of humor charged with irony. James Watson would later paint a portrait of her as unapproachable, which she certainly was to the people she did not like. On the other hand, her friends would describe her as loving and funny as anybody could be.

During this period, she and Raymond would work together on the structure of DNA, the molecule that carries genetic information. She used her knowledge of X-ray diffraction. Jacques had taught her to create images of the molecule, which helped in modeling its double helix structure. Rosalind leaned towards collecting data and completing the required calculations before coming to any conclusions about the structure. And so they did. By the end of 1952, she had the confirmation she needed. She wrote several papers about the discovery and sent them to the Scientific Journal dedicated to crystallography at the time before Francis Crick and James Watson had finished their model on March 6.

One fortunate—or unfortunate, depending on where one looks at it—day in January that year, Maurice showed the photograph of DNA crystals Rosalind and Raymond had produced to Watson without her knowledge or consent. Earlier that day, he had even gone so far as to dismiss her by saying she did not know how to correctly interpret her own data, to which she got understandably angry. They then used this information to develop their own model of the structure of DNA, which they published in the journal Nature in 1953. The publication made it seem as if Rosalind's papers were a confirmation of Watson and Crick's discoveries rather than an inspiration due to her data and the photograph 51. In 1962, Watson, Crick, and Wilkins would be awarded the Nobel Prize in Physiology or Medicine for the discovery of the double helix structure, and Rosalind would not even be mentioned.

In the middle of March, she transferred to Birkbeck College. A move she was not very happy about as the facilities were nowhere near as equipped or accommodating as those at King's College. There, she would continue her work on DNA for a while longer and start focusing on RNA and viruses. She and her team would publish several papers about these discoveries over the next five years.

During a trip to the US in 1956, Rosalind began to feel something odd in her stomach. She passed away two years later, on April 16, 1958, at the age of 37, from ovarian cancer after several relapses.

Despite the challenges she faced as a woman in science, Rosalind remained committed to her work and never let anyone look down on her. Her contributions to science were paramount, but her courage will be remembered forever.

Muriel Faye Siebert: Figures and Stocks

Muriel Faye Siebert was born in Cleveland, Ohio, on September 12th, 1932. Nicknamed Mickie—later "The First Lady of Wall Street"—she was the second child of a middle-class Jewish Hungarian family. Her father, Irwin, was a salesman, and her mother, Margaret, was a homemaker. Growing up, Mickie was a curious and ambitious child, eager to learn and explore, especially when it came to numbers and figures.

One auspicious day, she and two of her friends went on a vacation trip to New York and visited the New York Stock Exchange (NYSE). She marveled at the place and its dynamic, an experience that marked her for the rest of her life. And as it is found in the lives of other women in this book, this was Mickie's turning point.

She attended the then-called Western Reserve University in Cleveland, where she planned to study business and economics. Unfortunately, she was denied the degree by life circumstances when her father fell ill with cancer. Despite not having a college degree, she moved to New York City to pursue a much-desired career in finance two years after this event. She left with only $500 at the wheel of an old car but full of certainty.

Mickie's early years in New York were challenging. She faced discrimination at a time when being a secretary or support staffer was the only position women could aspire to in this male-dominated industry. She struggled to find work, which made her decide to lie about having a degree. She eventually landed a job as a junior analyst at Bache & Co. in 1954. From that moment on, she would jump between jobs because of the unfair pay gap with her colleagues. To her ears came the advice of a friend, who told her that to earn as much as men, she should buy a seat at the NYSE, a feat no other woman had ever achieved. During those months, she founded her own brokerage firm, Muriel Siebert & Co.

On December 28, 1967, Muriel made history when she became the first woman to purchase a seat on the NYSE. But it was not an easy journey; she needed a sponsor—male, of course, as there were no women there—which she got after several rejections and money for the cost of the seat itself. The amount was $445,000, an astronomical sum for the time, with $300,000 of it coming from a bank loan. That was the real challenge; it took her two years for a bank like Chase Manhattan to agree to the loan. Ten years would have to pass before we saw another woman in a seat.

Like many women in men's worlds, she had to develop a sharp tongue and a witty personality to gain respect. Everyday situations, like the apparent absence of a lady's room in the NYSE building, made her put in double the effort. The funny note was that there was a toilet for women, but nobody had bothered to tell her until her second year working there.

Success on Wall Street did not come into Mickie's life without personal sacrifice. She was known for her long hours and tireless work ethic, often working 16-hour days. Despite these challenges, she continued to make strides in her career. Her firm catered to small investors and provided them with access to the same services and opportunities that were available to larger investors.

In the following years, she was appointed Superintendent of Banks for the State of New York, ran in the Republican primary for the Senate seat of Daniel Patrick Moynihan, and in the 90s, her firm went public by reverse-merging with furniture holding company J. Michael & Sons.

Mickie's success in finance made her a trailblazer and role

model for women in business. She used her platform to advocate for greater inclusion of minorities in the workplace, serving on numerous boards and commissions and giving generously to charities and educational institutions. She would give much of her own money to different causes.

Even though she never married or had children, she would take her chihuahua dog, Monster Girl, to work. Monster Girl was the other member of her family, along with her sister.

She remained active in her business and philanthropic work until her death from cancer on August 24, 2013, at the age of 84. Her legacy lives on, inspiring generations of women and men to follow in her footsteps and work toward a more equitable and just society.

PERSEVERANCE AND PERSISTENCE AS STRATEGIES FOR BUILDING RESILIENCE

As said before, persistence is a choice, and probably the key element of our strategy is not to give up. It is closely connected to how we perceive and manage failures and setbacks and is what gives us a clear advantage to succeed in our dreams.

Now it would be pertinent to bring up a quote by Brené Brown (2017, p. 267): "There is no greater threat to the critics, cynics, and fearmongers than those of us who are willing to fall because we have learned how to rise." The women in this chapter had dreams, and not even the biggest of obstacles prevented them from achieving those dreams. They fell but stood up every time, and every time they did, it became easier.

Popular knowledge states that without persistence, defeat is certain, even before the start line. It takes a firm decision to go all in with our chosen pathway, and it does not matter how fast or slow the process is as long as we continue to move forward.

Another transcendent aspect of persistence is that it is a learned trait; in fact, it is a mindset that evolves into a habit. It develops in the presence of a strong desire to reach a certain goal, and it helps break through the vicious cycle of negative thoughts. But first, it helps in this process to pay attention to our discontent and longing before we focus on breaking negative thought habits. So, do not give up; you might be only one step away from your breakthrough.

And last but not least, we should never confuse "giving up on something" with "giving up a certain way" of doing something and finding a new way to get to our goal. Persistence is not blindly repeating the same action over and over again, knowing that it will not work. That is, by definition, insanity. Persistence is using all our efforts to find a new approach, either around, above, or under the obstacle; it does not matter as long as we move forward.

However, persistence at all costs comes with a risk. Cynicism is often observed when a woman enters a man's world, as Rosalind and Muriel experienced. The pitfall is to buy into this behavior and join in. Understanding that cynicism arises to mask inadequacy, anger, or feelings of threat can help navigate those situations without becoming complicit. And not complicit in, perhaps, hurting others, but complicit in hurting ourselves. And this is made evident by psychological research (Zainal & Newman, 2019): Cynical people have a greater chance of suffering from mental health concerns. This is something to consider.

Persistence in Rosalind and Muriel's Lives

When thinking about Rosalind's life, the first thought that may come to mind is the persistence and patience she must have had to collect all of the data she needed to come up with the discovery. Days and months of repeating the same lab tests, and when these did not work, finding a different approach and doing the necessary calculations to build a model that suited all the data. That is certainly something we must copy from her.

She went from place to place with just her goal in mind to do as much research as she could and not let anyone or anything take her down. She never strayed from her path and eventually got the answers she was looking for.

For Mickie, things were riskier if so. She left her hometown with almost no money and no college degree to give her some ground to stand on. The goal she had envisioned was so strong that she even went as far as to lie to try to get a job. She then faced discrimination and unfair treatment but took it as a growth factor. Humor lightened the difficult moments and dreams of doing things no other woman had ever done before, serving as the energy source for her unbreakable perseverance.

Exercise to Use Perseverance and Persistence as Strategies to Build Resilience

- Pay attention to your discontents and longings, reframe them, and form a strong desire toward your goal. Write down your desires and goals on a little card to keep in your pocket, and look at it as often as you need to. Make sure it is phrased in a positive way. Avoid writing what you do not want. Instead, write down in detail what it is that you desire. Do not be afraid to be specific.
- If you prefer, use the wonders of modern technology; set a recurring event in your calendar and let your phone remind you. The constant reminder and thought will trigger brain cell connections that will lead to reinforced desire and provide you with the necessary perseverance to not give up.

11

FACING THE UNKNOWN AND UNEXPECTED

Relinquish your attachment to the known, step into the unknown, and you will step into the field of all possibilities.
–Deepak Chopra

INTRODUCTION

Just as everything is connected in real life, so must be the concepts of this book. This chapter is about trust, but it is also about faith in our strength and resilience to overcome any challenge life throws at us.

We will learn how to understand the unknown and embrace the unexpected as part of our strategy to build a solid self.

This is the final strategy presented in this book and is also the only aspect that is a given in life. We re-frame unexpected challenges as another opportunity for learning and growth that otherwise might not present themselves.

On a personal note, I often look back at my past challenges and reflect on them; if I had not been exposed to a previous challenge in life, I would not have been prepared for the next one. Given a choice, I indeed would not have chosen the challenge myself, and in retrospect, destiny—if such a thing exists—presented itself as an inevitable learning curve on my journey.

Some of the women who inspired this chapter died tragically young, but they all impacted the lives of millions and left much for us to learn.

What Does It Mean to Expect?

According to the Merriam-Webster dictionary (n.d.), expect:

- "To consider probable or certain."
- "To consider reasonable, due, or necessary."
- "To consider bound in duty or obligated."
- "To anticipate or look forward to the coming or occurrence of."

For a little history, the root of the word "expect" is Latin *exspectare*, meaning "to look out for," which is a combination of ex- (a prefix meaning "out") + spectare ("to look").

To expect is to regard something as highly likely to happen or to regard someone as highly likely to be/do something. It is the belief in or anticipation of the arrival of a specific event.

Unexpected events happen constantly, and this is often what can crush our hopes and dreams if we are not resilient enough. Murphy's law makes a humorous attempt at describing the unexpected, simply put, as "Anything that can go wrong will go wrong, and at the worst possible time."

But as John Lennon famously said, "Life is what happens when we are busy making other plans" (BlewMinds, 2020). This is the essence of the unexpected, which is something that no one can anticipate or predict.

Building this into our strategy is vitally important to achieving success, and it depends on how we relate to our lives in the present moment.

THE WOMEN WHOSE LIVES TOOK AN UNEXPECTED TURN

Astrid Lindgren: A Character as Real as Its Impact

The grandmother of a generation of Swedish children, Astrid Anna Emilia Ericsson, was born on November 14th, 1907, in the small town of Vimmerby, Sweden. An idyllic farm with its matching idyllic red house was home for her parents, Samuel and Hanna, her four siblings, and her. The farm employed many people during the harvest season, and Astrid and her siblings would work alongside the workers, an experience that gave her a particular political view early on.

Astrid developed a wild imagination and a love for story-telling at a young age. She often created stories for her younger siblings, which would later inspire her writing.

At the age of 16 and having graduated from high school, she found a job at a local newspaper as a secretary and soon after began a relationship with her married boss, Reinhold Blomberg, who was thirty years older than her and was already the father of seven children. The affair resulted in a pregnancy, forcing her to move to Stockholm, and even though he proposed to her, she eventually declined. The judgment and gossiping had been too much for her to bear.

The new city gave her the opportunity to learn typing and stenography, but her salary as a newly hired secretary would not allow her to raise her child. So after much consideration, Astrid decided to travel to Denmark to give birth to her son, Lars. The boy was born on December 4, 1926, and was placed in the care of a foster family some weeks later. Despite the distance, she would save up as much as she could to travel often and see him.

The situation lasted for a few years until she could take the boy back to her home country. It was still financially difficult to raise him alone in Stockholm, so she decided to leave him with her parents. The boy's health was also delicate, which made an even stronger case for raising him in the countryside for a while. And the truth is that it was a happy place to grow up in as a child, just as it had been for Astrid and her siblings.

From 1928 on, she worked as a journalist and secretary for several individuals and organizations. At the Royal Automobile Club, she met the man who would later become her husband and father to her second child, Sture Lindgren. They got married in 1931—after he left his first wife for Astrid—and brought Lars to live with them. A little girl named Karin would come into the world three years later.

The years went by, and the idea of a character for a children's book began to take form in her head. Pippi Longstocking—her most transcendent character—was the result of her daughter's imagination and her eagerness to write, much like The Lord of The Rings was the result of the tales Tolkien told his children. In 1945, her first book about Pippi was published and became an instant success. The story of a young girl with superhuman strength and a love for adventure captured the hearts of children all around the world. Astrid went on to write numerous other children's books, many of which were also made into movies and TV shows. Her stories were known for their strong, independent female characters and their ability to tackle serious topics such as death, war, and discrimination in a way that was accessible and relatable to children.

Throughout her life, Astrid was a champion of human rights and social justice. One experience that marked her life was her trip to the US in 1948, where she was faced with the widespread racism and segregation of people of color. She was an opponent of nuclear weapons, an anti-imperialist, an advocate for animal rights, and a supporter of the women's movement. She received numerous awards and honors for her work, including the Hans Christian Andersen Medal and the Right Livelihood Award.

Sture passed away in 1952, a moment in which Astrid decided to fully commit to writing.

At some point, she concluded that the money she had earned was more than enough to live comfortably. A simple life surrounded by her loved ones was as much as she could ever ask for. Therefore, she started giving away the excess and helping causes she believed in.

Astrid passed away on January 28th, 2002, at the age of 94, in the same apartment she moved into with her family in 1941. Accompanying her were Karin and her grandchildren. Lars died too young in 1986.

Her words continue to inspire and delight children and adults alike, reminding us all of the power of imagination, courage, and kindness.

Ada Lovelace: The Girl With the Numbers

Augusta Ada Byron, Countess of Lovelace, came into the world on December 10, 1815, in London, England. The famous poet, Lord Byron, and his wife, Lady Annabella Byron—her maiden name was Milbanke—were her parents. The girl was born into a very privileged Victorian home, a setting—and a time, as it was the height of the industrial revolution—fit for a young science genius to thrive.

Lord Byron was quite the eccentric character, to say the least; Ada had many other illegitimate siblings from his affairs, and it is said that he engaged in relationships with both men and women, including an incestuous relationship with his half-sister. Ada never met him, as he abandoned her mother just a month after Ada's birth and England for good a few months later. Lord Byron finally died of illness in Greece when she was eight years old.

Lady Annabella, who was deeply concerned about the "volatile poetic insanity"—it was probably a mental illness—that seemed to run in the family, was determined to give her daughter a rigorous education in mathematics and logic to prevent her from developing any poetic tendencies—fields occupied almost exclusively by men. Ada showed a remarkable aptitude for numbers from a young age, and her distant and unloving mother *strongly* encouraged her to pursue her studies. Surprising to the prominent mathematicians of the period and male tutors of Ada, the mathematical gift came from her mother. But math was not the only subject she studied; her education included history, literature, languages, geography, music, and the more *girly* subjects of sewing and shorthand. And a practice far stranger for its foundations: Lying still for hours to learn self-control so as to never develop her father's impulses. We might be calling it meditation nowadays.

All the self-control would not be enough to prevent her from suffering strong and recurrent headaches or from contracting measles, a disease that forced her into bed for a year and brought her a temporary disability. At 16, she was walking again.

In 1833, Ada met Charles Babbage at his reception party, a renowned mathematician and inventor who had designed—and intended to impress his attendees with—a mechanical computing machine he named the Difference Engine. This first version of the machine would later go into oblivion due to a disagreement with the engineer building it and a lack of money. But something more important would remain from that night; Charles was impressed by Ada's intelligence and curiosity, and they became close friends and collaborators.

The improved second version of the machine, birthed in 1834, would be named the Analytical Engine, the first programmable general-purpose computer. In translating the article Italian Engineer Luigi Menabrea had written about Charles's machine, Ada added notes on what is now considered the first computer program to be executed, which was designed to calculate the Bernoulli numbers using the Analytical Engine. Her algorithm, which included loops and conditional branching, was far ahead of its time and laid the groundwork for modern computer programming. Ada was the first person to recognize that the Analytical Engine could be used to perform calculations beyond just numbers, such as creating music and graphics. The complete translated scientific article would be published under a pseudonym in 1843.

Ada married thirty-year-old aristocrat William King, a friend of her mother's, at the age of 19. He was a decent and supportive husband, a perfect complement to someone like her. Their social circle was as high as names like Charles Dickens and Michael Faraday could be. They had three children together: Byron, Anne Isabella, and Ralph Gordon. During the time between her first and last pregnancy—from 1835 to 1839—she had to put the study and development of the Analytical Engine aside. On top of her existing health problems, Ada contracted Cholera in 1837, a disease that left her with respiratory and digestive aftereffects. The doctor prescribed laudanum, an opiate, to deal with the pain. The addictive remedy would bring forth another set of aftereffects.

Just like her father did, and just like her mother's worst nightmare, Ada had scandals of her own. Rumors of affairs with other men and gambling problems made the last years of her life not as quiet as they could have been.

Ada's cinematic life was cut short on November 27th, 1852, at the age of 36, when she fell ill from terminal uterine cancer. Her last desire was to be buried alongside her father.

Her contributions to computer science and mathematics were largely forgotten for many years, but her legacy has since been recognized. Ada Lovelace is remembered as a brilliant mathematician, a visionary thinker, and a pioneer in the field of computer science whose contributions continue to inspire future generations of scientists and innovators.

Princess Diana: The Heart of a Kingdom

Princess Diana, Lady Di, the People's Princess, was born on July 1st, 1961, in Sandringham, England. Diana Frances Spencer was the fourth of five children of John and Frances, Viscount, and Viscountess Althorp. But just like it happened to many of the women on these pages, her brother John—a year older than Diana—would pass away shortly after his birth. As a child, she would spend her days with her siblings at the family home in Park House, Norfolk, England. Given her noble status, she was in contact with the royal family and many other noble families.

Despite her privileged upbringing, Diana's childhood was not always happy. Her parents' difficult, unloving marriage and eventual divorce—at Diana's age of six—were the main cause for her feeling abandoned and lonely. Both of them cared little about spending time with their children; they were, perhaps, the standard examples of distant parents one could come across in a film or TV show. At nine years old, Diana was sent to Riddlesworth Hall, a boarding school for girls, and three years later, to West Heath Girls' School, where her sisters were enrolled. Among the activities she enjoyed the most were swimming, diving, ballet, and tap dancing. But she particularly excelled in music, with piano as her main interest. She had a lovely singing voice as well, but her shyness kept her from auditioning for the choir.

Frances went on to marry Peter Shand Kydd, a wealthy heir to a wallpaper company. John would remarry as well, to a famous novelist's daughter by the name of Raine McCorquodale. The children found out about the event through the newspapers. And they would not have it easy to care for their new stepmother, whom they blamed for their family's destruction.

At sixteen years old, she would meet the then 30-year-old Prince Charles for the first time. Even though he was dating her older sister Sarah—the relationship would not last long—he was charmed by Diana's beauty and personality.

After turning 18 and graduating from high school, she began working as a kindergarten teacher, a nanny, and a few other low-paying jobs. Children were the passion of her life.

By that time, Prince Charles had been dating several women, including Camilla Rosemary Shand, who would later become his wife. With the pressure from the Queen and his surroundings to get married to somebody other than Camilla—whom she deemed unfit—Prince Charles began a courtship with Diana that lasted no more than 13 dates. He proposed to her on February 6, 1981. The story captivated the world.

For Diana, the interview the couple did after the engagement would be the turning point in her life. In the video of the broadcast, the reporter commented that they looked very much in love, to which the Prince would reply with a chuckle, "Whatever love means." Perhaps this was the moment she realized fairy tales were only printed on a book page. Their wedding, held on July 29, 1981, could be called the stage of a fairy tale that came to life and was followed live by millions of people around the world. It would be the worst day of her life.

Not long after the wedding, Diana found out about her husband's affair with then Camilla Parker-Bowles—she had married a wealthy man—an issue that broke her heart. She was so desperate and lonely that she threatened to kill herself and later threw herself off a staircase; she was pregnant at the moment. Everybody came running to her aid except for the Prince. The pressure to be a perfect princess to the outside world and her awful marriage took a great toll on her mental health, causing her to develop bulimia. Despite the signs and symptoms, the royal family would still treat her like a child with a whim. There is nothing worse for a sick person than to be told, "You are exaggerating."

As a member of the royal family, Diana was expected to carry out public duties and participate in charitable work with a smile. She soon became known for her warmth and compassion, particularly in her work with children and those affected by HIV/AIDS.

On June 21, 1982, Diana gave birth to her first son, Prince William, the future king.

The following years were marked by affairs from both parties. She started a relationship with a cavalry officer named James Hewitt. This is thought to have happened before Prince Harry, who was born on September 15, 1984. Naturally, people began questioning if he was, in fact, his son and not Prince Charles's. James denied this rumor in an interview and added that he had met Diana two years after Prince Harry's birth.

In her role as a mother, Diana wanted her children to have experiences closer to working-class people. For this reason, she would take them to amusement parks, go shopping, and buy them fast food. Not only that, but she would take them to homeless shelters to lend a hand. It was not an activity their father was very pleased about.

A few years after her first affair, Diana started a relationship with her bodyguard, Barry Mannakee. She claimed it was only a very good friendship, while others doubted that. But the result would be the same, his dismissal. And only a few months later, he was killed in a motorcycle accident, with the tragic news coming from her husband, no less, in a very casual way. She thought Barry was killed on purpose.

By that point, Diana had already decided to do everything she could to get a divorce, something that would undoubtedly be difficult. To achieve this, she needed to make the public stand by her side. She spoke to a journalist about the royal family and would do so in subsequent interviews over the following years. In 1992, the couple announced their separation, and their divorce was finalized in 1996, with shared custody of their children.

During these four years, both of them continued to see other people. Among them was Dodi Al-Fayed, an Egyptian millionaire and movie producer whom Diana fell in love with. His family was the owner of the internationally known Harrods Department Store. To the paparazzi and much of the public, he was just a playboy, and the fact that he was Muslim played a big role in enlarging all prejudices.

Despite the turmoil in her personal life, Diana remained a beloved public figure. She was involved in countless charities, including the Landmine Survivors Network and the British Red Cross, and her humanitarian work earned her the nickname "The Queen of Hearts." She was feeling happy for the first time in a long time.

The couple was planning on getting married someday, and some people thought she was pregnant at the moment of her accident. A Muslim half-sibling in the royal family would have been unprecedented. She was also planning to reveal more secrets about the royal family—some of those secrets we have come to know in recent years with a certain Prince Andrew and a certain Jeffrey Epstein at their center.

Tragedy struck on August 31, 1997, when Diana and Dodi were killed in a car crash in Paris. The news of her death sent shockwaves around the world, and millions mourned the loss of a woman who had touched so many lives. But some doubts also arose from the circumstances of her death in a Paris tunnel, where there were cameras but none functioning at the moment of her crash. The official narrative was that the cars chasing her were paparazzi. Despite this, it came out later that she had written a letter to her butler saying that her ex-husband wanted her dead. Several investigations were carried out throughout the years to determine what had happened, but all came to the conclusion that it was an accident. Until the most recent one, the seat belts were damaged, and the ambulance took an unjustifiably long time to take her to the hospital. All these details add to the theory that she was, in fact, killed by the British secret services. For the moment, the questions remain.

In death, Diana's legacy only grew. Her commitment to charitable work and her compassion for others inspired countless people to follow in her footsteps, including her two sons, Prince William and Prince Harry, who continue to do her work today. The strength in her to face power remains a beacon for all women across the world.

UNDERSTANDING THE UNKNOWN AND EMBRACING THE UNEXPECTED

Life is a mystery; no human has all the answers. In this way, the *unknown* is the one thing we know with certainty is out there, and to fear it is only natural. The question we should ask ourselves is, "Why are we so worried about the unknown? Is it that we constantly expect a negative result?"

On the other hand, some people thrive in uncertain times. For those of us who do not, we are left wondering how and if that is possible for us as well. Maybe we believe that we can control uncertainty, but if we are honest, failure seems inevitable. Maybe our failure manifests itself by running away from uncertainty. All of these are valid responses to the unknown, but not all produce the same outcomes.

Research (Vaish et al., 2008) has shown that being aware of and expecting a negative event or challenge is a human evolutionary advantage, as it helps us develop a response pattern and come up with a possible solution (Carretié et al., 2001). Understanding that the unknown is a part of life will mitigate the anxiety that comes with it. In fact, the unknown and unexpected can be a gift to us, and it is up to us to find the treasure. We can also take it as a guide for our journey; life is happening *for* us, not *to* us. Then, in the words of a very close friend of mine: "What is this unexpected situation here to teach me?"

All this leads to the conclusion that unknown, unexpected adversity is essential for our growth. It helps us trigger our creativity, puts our skills to the test, and prepares us for the next chapter in our lives. In some ways, it forces us to become better.

Let's state the truth for a moment. Most of us, if given a choice, would not choose any challenging situation; we probably prefer to stay in our comfort zone and play along. But that is not what life is about. We are here to grow and expand ourselves, creating our best possible version. Heroes are rarely born sitting on the couch watching Netflix; they are born in the midst of the most challenging situations and facing adversity.

Adversities are our friends, not our enemies. It can feel overwhelming, but we must trust that there is a reward hidden in it somewhere, just waiting for us to discover it. Be open to the unknown and unexpected, even if it is a painful challenge, which it will probably be at some point.

Certainly, this is easier said than done, but with the faith in ourselves, persistence, perseverance, and self-compassion we have developed throughout this written journey, we now have the capability to look at obstacles and find the bright side in them, embracing our vulnerabilities. In other words, this is how we work on our resilience.

Three Women Making the Best of the Unexpected

The unexpected event in Astrid's life took the form of a pregnancy at an all-too-young age. But it also came with immense doses of love. She had so much love that she had to make difficult decisions for the sake of her baby. She overcame the fear and kept pushing through. Her character, Pippi, is the embodiment of pushing through the hardest of unexpected situations. We can even pose ourselves the following question: Would Pippi be the character that she is if Astrid had not gone through the uncertain events she went through? The answer is unknown.

Ada lived a meaningful life that could have been three before her unexpected death. We must learn from her to live every day of ours as if it were the last one. It's cliché, but true nonetheless. Think every day, "What would I want to do if this were my last day on Earth?"

For Diana, the unexpected came when she realized her future husband did not love her. She was a believer in love, and that broke her. At first, married life was difficult for her, but soon she embraced the situation she was in, giving all her love to her children and other children, to people in need, and to those who had close to nothing. In the process, she even found true love.

Small Exercise to Embrace the Unknown and Unexpected and Grow Resilience

This next exercise has some magic to it. Queen Elizabeth II said that taking a breath when facing challenging times, or in Latin, *inspirare*, is like having "inspiration."

- The next time something you did not expect—an adverse event—happens, take a deep breath in and hold it for three seconds. Repeat this three times. Then gather your thoughts and put your emotional responses on hold, especially those of stress or sadness. Make an appointment time for those emotions; if you like, book a "pity party" in three days where you will allow these emotions to come. But for now, write down on paper the following: "I want to take all the benefits and all the learnings from this situation." Think about it, what could the lessons be, and what good could come out of this?

FINAL THOUGHTS

THE (WOMEN'S) SECRET TO NOT GIVING UP

Integrity is choosing courage over comfort; choosing what is right over what is fun, fast, or easy; and choosing to practice our values rather than simply professing them.
–Brené Brown

Integrity and Gratitude

Integrity is our final stage in the process of building resilience. We can break down this characteristic into its constituent elements: honesty, trustworthiness, consistency, fairness, accountability, and ethical behavior. It involves having values and upholding them courageously, being honest with ourselves and others, and having gratitude for the kindness, support, and expected and unexpected opportunities to learn life throws at us.

We can say that gratitude and integrity go hand in hand and reinforce each other. Practicing gratitude enhances our commitment to living with integrity, while integrity deepens our sense of gratitude and appreciation for the positive aspects of our lives. If we act with integrity, we feel grateful for the contributions of others, and in turn, we make our own contributions to the world.

Integrity can be learned but needs to be practiced and upheld. Gratitude along the way makes it a more meaningful and fulfilling experience.

Gratitude

The biggest word amongst them all, not only because it contains the highest vibration within or because being grateful makes us happy, but because it is the perfect combination of words. It contains two Latin words in it: One is *gratus,* which means "pleasing" or "thankful," and in a later period the word *tudo* was attached, meaning "all." Being thankful for all, being thankful to all, or being thankful for all. In Italian and Spanish, it is still in daily use as *grazie di tutto,* and *gracias* as the common word for thank you. It is similar to the use we give to the word *grace,* with its nature originally being "filled with God's favor."

Thinking of the word puts an instant smile on my face. When I think of things I am grateful for, I can feel it in my body somewhere in between my tummy and heart. When I can generate a moment of gratitude within, it feels as if my body is seeking a connection to the source of all beings.

Gratitude is the key element for all human beings; it puts things into perspective, reminds us of where we come from and where we are going, unites us with other beings, and centers our attention on the small things, which essentially are the big things of life—it sums things up as being part of a *bigger picture.*

The word gratitude and its meaning do not stand alone, though; they have companions: compassion and contribution. Without compassion or contributions, there is no such thing as gratitude. It is almost as if these three words are in constant play, like wind chimes, contrasting and complementing each other at the same time.

When you experience gratitude for and within yourself, there is no room left for feelings of giving up. The feeling of giving up is a mixture of anxiety, overwhelming powerlessness, and shame. In any situation, if we open ourselves to gratitude, we will be thankful for the opportunity for growth and learning. Cultivating gratitude is the antidote to giving up.

So, hold on and do not give up; you might just be one step away from where you envisioned yourself—just one step away from success.

Failure along the way is inevitable and is an important part of everyone's success story. It not only tells us that we found a way that does not work but that we are on our journey to figuring out a way that does work. If there are people who have not failed, it is because they have not tried. Failure and obstacles are qualifiers to help us get better at what we do; they prepare us in better ways for what is ahead.

Do not lose your faith and beliefs because others might criticize you or withdraw their support. It is easy to give up when you feel alone or experience uncertainty and anxiety on your journey. Other people do not know what you know; they cannot see what you see in your vision, so they might not be able to join you or follow you. However, failure is a crucial point within the process; it is a sign of progress. Have faith and reassure yourself that you are going toward your goal.

What Curtis L. Carlson said and used as his family credo beautifully sums up the chapters in this book in one sentence— it is still today the leitmotiv of the Carlson Family Foundation: "Whatever you do, do it with integrity. Wherever you go, go as a leader. Whoever you serve, serve with care. Whenever you dream, dream with your all—and never, ever give up."

When we started this journey, I talked about the reason for writing this book and shared my personal wonderings leading to the lines in front of you. This work is an homage and a demonstration of gratitude to the remarkable women here and everywhere.

By now, hopefully, the stories of the marvelous women in this book have had a positive impact on giving you perspective, inspiration, and strategies. And not only inspiration and company for women but also for men—and I am referring to you too, my dear male friends.

Sometimes, representation is not about how we look on the outside but how we connect on a deeper level, how we face challenges and come out stronger, and what we give the world in the process. Is there a gender for courage or compassion? Is there a skin color for honesty? Do we all need to look alike to form a network of support? Are faith and passion a luxury only for the wealthy? Do our values need to clash depending on the national border that contains us?

I would like to believe these pages showed that inspiration can come to us in any form or shape and from anyone. It is about knowing what the story means in your heart, not only in your mind. Having that connection and identifying with these women will hopefully help you actively pursue these strategies by owning them, using them, and spilling wisdom onto them. Resilience does not have one single road to get there, and creativity is our ally.

So, the goal is not only to be a useful book but to encourage you to generously share the learnings and elements that resonated. To provide a timeless source of wisdom, contribute to common knowledge, and give voice to unheard women in history. And with any luck, in an entertaining fashion.

There are countless more women out there who shaped the

world we now live in, and I would like to encourage you to go and find out about them. But meaningful women are not only those who are famous. And as my dear colleague Dr. Rebecca taught, they can be anyone, from our mothers, daughters, sisters, and best friends to our neighbors. They can be us; we all have stories to share. So, please do! Do not hesitate to write and tell me an inspiring story about you or anyone around you.

REFERENCES

Abad, A. F. (2021, August 2). *Alice Milliat, la remadora que desafió al COI para que las mujeres pudieran ir a los Juegos Olímpicos. S Moda EL PAÍS.* https:// smoda.elpais.com/placeres/alice-milliat-pionera-deporte-femenino-juegos-olimpicos-coi/

ABC News (Australia). (2013). *"Tell me who": Negus reflects on Thatcher reverse grilling* [Video]. YouTube. https://www.youtube.com/watch?v=imWJZQQv P1w&ab_channel=ABCNews%28Australia%29

Academy of Achievement. (2016). *Justice Ruth Bader Ginsburg, Academy Class of 1995, Full Interview* [Video]. YouTube. https://www.youtube.com/watch?v= YCH32n7drMc&ab_channel=AcademyofAchievement

Agency, C. (2019, April 2). *Women Who Rocked the Finance World — Muriel Faye "Mickie" Siebert.* Medium. https://contentworks.medium.com/women-who-rocked-the-finance-world-muriel-faye-mickie-siebert-556800ddf2f8

Alexander, K. L. (2019). *Muriel Siebert.* National Women's History Museum. https://www.womenshistory.org/education-resources/biographies/muriel-siebert

Alexander, K. L. (2020). *Ruth Bader Ginsburg.* National Women's History Museum. https://www.womenshistory.org/education-resources/biographies/ruth-bader-ginsburg

American Academy of Achievement. (2007). *Nora Ephron, Academy Class of 2007, Full Interview* [Video]. YouTube. https://www.youtube.com/watch?v=3HhXg Lux6iw&t=1405s&ab_channel=AcademyofAchievement

American Academy of Achievement. (2009). *Dame Jane Goodall.* Academy of Achievement. https://achievement.org/achiever/jane-goodall/#interview

American Masters PBS. (2020). *Bessie Coleman: First African American Aviator | Unladylike2020 | American Masters | PBS* [Video]. YouTube. https://www. youtube.com/watch?v=4fSwHryVWZE&ab_channel=AmericanMastersPBS

American Psychological Association. (2020). *APA Dictionary of Psychology "social support."* Dictionary.apa.org. https://dictionary.apa.org/social-support

American Psychological Association. (2021). *Perseverance Toward Life Goals Can Fend Off Depression, Anxiety, Panic Disorders.* Apa.org. https://www.apa.org/ news/press/releases/2019/05/goals-perseverance

American Psychological Association. (2022). *APA Dictionary of Psychology "resilience."* Dictionary.apa.org. https://dictionary.apa.org/resilience

American Psychological Association. (n.d.-a). *APA Dictionary of Psychology "belief."* Dictionary.apa.org. https://dictionary.apa.org/belief

American Psychological Association. (n.d.-b). *APA Dictionary of Psychology "compassion."* Dictionary.apa.org. https://dictionary.apa.org/compassion

American Psychological Association. (n.d.-c). *APA Dictionary of Psychology "courage."* Dictionary.apa.org. https://dictionary.apa.org/courage

American Psychological Association. (n.d.-d). *APA Dictionary of Psychology "faith."* Dictionary.apa.org. https://dictionary.apa.org/faith

American Psychological Association. (n.d.-e). *APA Dictionary of Psychology "honesty."* Dictionary.apa.org. https://dictionary.apa.org/honesty

American Psychological Association. (n.d.-f). *APA Dictionary of Psychology "kindness."* Dictionary.apa.org. https://dictionary.apa.org/kindness

American Psychological Association. (n.d.-g). *APA Dictionary of Psychology "passion."* Dictionary.apa.org. https://dictionary.apa.org/passion

American Psychological Association. (n.d.-h). *APA Dictionary of Psychology "persistence."* Dictionary.apa.org. https://dictionary.apa.org/persistence

American Psychological Association. (n.d.-i). *APA Dictionary of Psychology "value."* Dictionary.apa.org. https://dictionary.apa.org/value

American Psychological Association. (n.d.-j). *APA Dictionary of Psychology "vision."* Dictionary.apa.org. https://dictionary.apa.org/vision

American Psychological Association. (n.d.-k). *APA Dictionary of Psychology "vulnerability."* Dictionary.apa.org. https://dictionary.apa.org/vulnerability

Aprendemos Juntos 2030. (2018). *Versión Completa. Resiliencia: el dolor es inevitable, el sufrimiento es opcional. Boris Cyrulnik* [Video]. YouTube. https://www.youtube.com/watch?v=_IugzPwpsyY&list=TLPQMDQwNDIwMjPV9RKPZ9EdaA&index=3&ab_channel=AprendemosJuntos2030

Aprendemos Juntos 2030. (2019). *Versión Completa. Lecciones de vida de un espíritu indomable. Jane Goodall, primatóloga* [Video]. YouTube. https://www.youtube.com/watch?v=HnGKvC4iDG0&ab_channel=AprendemosJuntos2030

Aprendemos Juntos 2030. (2020). *V. Completa. "¿Te han dicho que no encajas? Ponte unas zapatillas y corre". Kathrine Switzer, atleta* [Video]. YouTube. https://www.youtube.com/watch?v=srPhefQ4nsk&ab_channel=AprendemosJuntos2030

Asian Eye. (2007). *The Light and Legacy of Dr. Fe Del Mundo* [Video]. YouTube. https://www.youtube.com/watch?v=ZVyH6skgKh4&ab_channel=ChitoReyes

Astrid Lindgren Company. (2023). *Childhood.* Astridlindgren. https://www.astridlindgren.com/en/about-astrid-lindgren/childhood

Astronautix. (2008, March 25). *Tereshkova.* Web.archive.org. https://web.archive.org/web/20080325163329/http://www.astronautix.com/astros/terhkova.htm

Austen, J. (1813). *Pride and Prejudice.* Salem Press. https://www.amazon.com/Pride-Prejudice-Jane-Austen/dp/8172344503

Bartley, P. (2002). *Emmeline Pankhurst* (1st ed.). Routledge. https://www.amazon.com/Pankhurst-Routledge-Historical-Biographies-Paperback/dp/B011DC1IK4

BBC News. (2002, September 21). Hewitt denies Prince Harry link. *News.bbc.co.uk.* http://news.bbc.co.uk/2/hi/uk_news/2273498.stm

BBC News. (2014). *Boston Marathon: Meet the first woman to run it* [Video]. YouTube.https://www.youtube.com/watch?v=aO2ChjVGL7c&list= TLPQMTcwMzIwMjPptdfwc_DPVA&index=3&ab_channel=BBCNews

BBC. (2019, December 25). *BBC - History - British History in depth: Florence Nightingale: the Lady with the Lamp.* Web.archive.org. https://web.archive.org/web/20191225134336/http://www.bbc.co.uk/history/british/victorians/nightin gale_01.shtml

Beckett, C. (2006). *Thatcher.* Haus. https://www.jstor.org/stable/j.ctt1hhfnfw

Bergan, R. (2012, June 27). Nora Ephron obituary. *The Guardian.* https://www.theguardian.com/film/2012/jun/27/nora-ephron

Best of Humans. (2020). *The Very Best of Nora Ephron (w/ Tom Hanks, Mike Nichols, Rob Reiner)* [Video]. YouTube. https://www.youtube.com/watch?v=mCBd WwnGDhs&ab_channel=BestofHumans

Betsi Cadwaladr, Bala Crimean War nurse, given memorial. (2012, August 1). *BBC News.* https://www.bbc.com/news/uk-wales-19075075

Bible Hub. (2017, July 18). *Strong's Greek: 3958. πάσχω, (paschó) -- to suffer, to be acted on.* Web.archive.org. https://web.archive.org/web/20170718232618/http://biblehub.com/greek/3958.htm

Biblioteca Nacional de Uruguay. (2021). *Ciclo "Letra de mujer" - Paulina Luisi por Facundo Ponce de León* [Video]. YouTube. https://www.youtube.com/watch?v= ZyN16sIsdjA&ab_channel=BibliotecaNacionaldeUruguay

Binkowski, B. (2017, March 6). *Was Coco Chanel a Nazi Spy?* Snopes. https://www.snopes.com/news/2017/03/06/coco-chanel-nazi-spy/

Biografías Épicas. (2020). *Biografía ASTRID LINDGREN - LA CREADORA DE PIPPI CALZASLARGAS* [Video]. YouTube. https://www.youtube.com/watch?v= 3k1Nb61b4Hc&t=11s&ab_channel=Biograf%C3%ADAs%C3%89picas

Biographics. (2018a). *Ada Lovelace: The First Computer Programmer* [Video]. YouTube. https://www.youtube.com/watch?v=IZptxisyVqQ&list=TLPQMj MwNDIwMjPwshEIyPvWrQ&index=3&ab_channel=Biographics

Biographics. (2018b). *Amelia Earhart: A Record Setting Pilot* [Video]. YouTube. https://www.youtube.com/watch?v=tjTSMMnxDZk&ab_channel= Biographics

Biographics. (2018c). *Jane Goodall: Living with Chimpanzees* [Video]. YouTube. https://www.youtube.com/watch?v=JqWms8Rl6u4&ab_channel= Biographics

Biographics. (2018d). *Marie Curie: A Life of Sacrifice and Achievement* [Video].YouTube.https://www.youtube.com/watch?v=AFjGrVVXuvU&list=TLPQMjcw MzIwMjNAzKxDLVbjEA&index=4&ab_channel=Biographics

Biographics. (2018e). *Princess Diana: Her Life and Mysterious Death* [Video]. YouTube. https://www.youtube.com/watch?v=A_u9Zs5WTCE&ab_chan nel=Biographics

Biographics. (2019a). *Coco Chanel: Fashion Designer, Business Mogul, and Spy.* YouTube. https://www.youtube.com/watch?v=eeLndkDbQlw&ab_channel= Biographics

Biographics. (2019b). *Eleanor Roosevelt - The First Lady to the World* [Video]. YouTube. https://www.youtube.com/watch?v=MpI6In4fmeo&ab_channel= Biographics

Biographics. (2019c). *Florence Nightingale - The Lady with the Lamp* [Video]. YouTube. https://www.youtube.com/watch?v=E-97fnUAbyo&ab_channel= Biographics

Biographics. (2020a). *Margaret Thatcher: Britain's Greatest Prime Minister… or its Worst?* [Video]. YouTube. https://www.youtube.com/watch?v=bjiczzsv5IQ& list=TLPQMTcwMzIwMjNXthk01RElAQ&index=5&ab_channel= Biographics

Biographics. (2020b). *Rosa Parks: Activist. Fighter. Hero* [Video]. YouTube. https:// www.youtube.com/watch?v=NYlBVVYVJmQ&ab_channel=Biographics

Biography Editors. (2021, May 6). *Ada Lovelace - Quotes, Children & Facts.* Biography. https://www.biography.com/scholars-educators/ada-lovelace

Biography. (2019, April 22). *Coco Chanel - Fashion, Quotes & Facts - Biography.* Web.archive.org. https://web.archive.org/web/20190422153514/https:// www.biography.com/fashion-designer/coco-chanel

Biography. (2020). *Margaret Thatcher: First Female Prime Minister of Britain | Mini Bio | Biography* [Video]. YouTube. https://www.youtube.com/watch?v=JPpSBg Hu_TU&list=TLPQMTcwMzIwMjNXthk01RElAQ&index=3&ab_channel= Biography

BlewMinds. (2020, June 26). *Life happens when you're busy making other plans | Blew-Minds Consulting.* BlewMinds. https://blewminds.com/musings/squad-musings/life-is-what-happens-when-youre-busy-making-other-plans-john-lennon/#:~:text=John%20Lennon-

Bobby, L. M. (2020, September 21). *Being Honest With Yourself.* Growing Self. https://www.growingself.com/being-honest-with-yourself/

Bradford, S., & Internet Archive. (2006). *Diana.* In Internet Archive. New York : Viking. https://archive.org/details/diana00sara/page/n9/mode/2up

Brené, B. (2018). *Dare to lead : brave work, tough conversations, whole hearts.* Random House Large Print Publishing. https://www.amazon.com/Dare-Lead-Brave-Conversations-Hearts/dp/1785042149

Brinkley, D. (2000). *Rosa Parks.* Archive.nytimes. https://archive.nytimes.com/ www.nytimes.com/books/first/b/brinkley-parks.html

Brockes, E., & @emmabrockes. (2007, March 3). Everything is copy. *The Guardian.* https://www.theguardian.com/books/2007/mar/03/fiction

Brown, B. (2010). *The gifts of imperfection: let go of who you think you're supposed to be and embrace who you are.* Hazelden. https://www.amazon.com/Gifts-Imperfec-tion-Think-Supposed-Embrace/dp/159285849X

Brown, B. (2013, January 15). *Shame vs. Guilt.* https://brenebrown.com/articles/

2013/01/15/shame-v-guilt/

Brown, B. (2017). *Rising strong : how the ability to reset transforms the way we live, love, parent, and lead.* Random House. https://www.amazon.com/gp/product/0812995821/

Brown, B. (2018, October 15). *Clear Is Kind. Unclear Is Unkind.* https://brenebrown.com/articles/2018/10/15/clear-is-kind-unclear-is-unkind/

Brown, B. (n.d.). *The Gifts of Imperfection | Faith is a place of mystery where we find the courage to believe in what we cannot see.* Retrieved July 6, 2023, from https://brenebrown.com/art/tgoi-faith/

Bueno, D., Elizalde, I., Mangado, M. P., Sarlo, S., & Soust, L. (2005). *Documental Paulina Luisi* [Video]. YouTube. https://www.youtube.com/watch?v=0LAFjAOQROA&list=TLPQMDgwNDIwMjMOfcb6EuGKKg&index=4&ab_channel=Mar%C3%ADaPazMangado

Burgess, C., & Hall, R. (2009). *The first Soviet cosmonaut team : their lives and legacies.* Praxis. https://www.amazon.com/First-Soviet-Cosmonaut-Team-Legacies/dp/0387848231

Butler, S. (2009). *East to the dawn : the life of Amelia Earhart.* Da Capo Press. https://www.amazon.com/East-Dawn-Life-Amelia-Earhart/dp/030681837X

Campbell, J. (2000). *Margaret Thatcher.* Jonathan Cape. https://www.amazon.com/Margaret-Thatcher-Iron-Lady-v/dp/0099516772

Carpentier, F., Castan-Vicente, F., & Nicolas, C. (2020). *Women Sport Leaders during the Twentieth Century.* Encyclopédie d'Histoire Numérique de L'Europe. https://ehne.fr/en/encyclopedia/themes/gender-and-europe/earning-a-living/women-sport-leaders-during-twentieth-century

Carretié, L., Mercado, F., Tapia, M., & Hinojosa, J. A. (2001). Emotion, attention, and the "negativity bias", studied through event-related potentials. *International Journal of Psychophysiology, 41*(1), 75–85. https://doi.org/10.1016/s0167-8760(00)00195-1

Cavallaro, U. (2017). *Women spacefarers : sixty different paths to space.* Springer ; Chichester, Uk. https://www.amazon.com/Women-Spacefarers-Different-Springer-Praxis/dp/3319340476

CBS Boston. (2016). *A Boston Marathon First: Bobbi Gibb On Her History-Making Run* [Video]. YouTube. https://www.youtube.com/watch?v=W8yKILypImQ&t=37s&ab_channel=CBSBoston

CBS Mornings. (2016). *Ruth Bader Ginsburg in her own words* [Video]. YouTube. https://www.youtube.com/watch?v=JzXX-7xaYzA&ab_channel=CBSMornings

CBS News. (1999). *Muriel Siebert - 1st Woman To Hold Seat On The New York Stock Exchange (1999) #economy #money* [Video]. YouTube. https://www.youtube.com/watch?v=T8ZQrAGWbwo&ab_channel=TheEconomicsArchives

Chaney, L. (2011). *Coco Chanel: An Intimate Life.* Penguin. https://www.amazon.com/Coco-Chanel-Intimate-Lisa-Chaney/dp/0143122126

Chen, R. (2017, July 24). *The Real Meaning of Passion.* Embrace Possibility. https://

www.embracepossibility.com/blog/real-meaning-passion/

Chua, P. S. (2011). *An Icon Passes Away*. The Far Eastern University. https://www. feu-alumni.com/announcements/fdm.htm

Clauss-Ehlers, C. S. (2010). *Cultural Resilience*. Encyclopedia of Cross-Cultural School Psychology, 324–326. https://doi.org/10.1007/978-0-387-71799-9_115

Cloninger, C. R., Svrakic, D. M., & Przybeck, T. R. (1993). A psychobiological model of temperament and character. *Archives of General Psychiatry, 50*(12), 975–990. https://doi.org/10.1001/archpsyc.1993.01820240059008

Colpitts, G., & Devine, H. (2017). *Finding Directions West: Readings that Locate and Dislocate Western Canada's Past*. University of Calgary Press. https://prism.ucal gary.ca/server/api/core/bitstreams/d90c2774-b474-4feb-a12e-75cb4708a809/content

Cook, G. (2013, November 12). The Moral Life of Babies. *Scientific American*. https://www.scientificamerican.com/article/the-moral-life-of-babies/

Corporación de Radio y Televisión Española. (2018, March 10). *Mujeres viajeras - Alexandra David Néel- Madame Tibet*. rtve.es. https://www.rtve.es/play/videos/ mujeres-viajeras/mujeres-viajeras-alexandra-david-neel-madame-tibet/ 4513924/

Date un Vlog. (2017). *#10 Biografías científicas - Marie Curie, una mujer sin barreras* [Video]. YouTube. https://www.youtube.com/watch?v=0Fh2Nw_W_UU& list=TLPQMjcwMzIwMjNAzKxDLVbjEA&index=5&ab_channel= DateunVlog

David-Néel, A. (n.d.). *Showing all quotes that contain "Suffering rises up those souls that are truly great"*. Goodreads. https://www.goodreads.com/quotes/search? utf8=%E2%9C%93&q=Suffering+rises+up+those+souls+that+are+ truly+great&commit=Search

David-Néel, A., & Yongden, A. A. (1967). *The secret oral teachings in Tibetan Buddhist sects*. City Lights Books. https://www.amazon.com/Secret-Teachings-Tibetan-Buddhist-Sects/dp/1684220718

Dawson, V. P., & Bowles, M. D. (2005). *Realizing the Dream of Flight*. NASA History Division. https://www.amazon.com/Realizing-Dream-Flight-Biographical-Centennial/dp/1470020505

De Saint-Exupéry, A. (1943). *The Little Prince*. Ancient Wisdon Publications. https://www.amazon.com/Little-Prince-Antoine-Saint-Exup%C3%A9ry/dp/0156012197

Death Penalty Information Center. (2020, January 20). *The Reverend Dr. Martin Luther King, Jr.: "Hate cannot drive out hate; only love can do that."* https://death penaltyinfo.org/news/the-reverend-dr-martin-luther-king-jr-hate-cannot-drive-out-hate-only-love-can-do-that

Decety, J., & Michalska, K. J. (2009). Neurodevelopmental changes in the circuits underlying empathy and sympathy from childhood to adulthood.

Developmental Science, 13(6), 886–899. https://doi.org/10.1111/j.1467-7687. 2009.00940.x

Dejevsky, M. (2017, March 29). The first woman in space: "People shouldn't waste money on wars." *The Guardian.* https://www.theguardian.com/global-development-professionals-network/2017/mar/29/valentina-tereshkova-first-woman-in-space-people-waste-money-on-wars

DEPORTV. (2020). *Alice Milliat, luchadora que bregó por mujeres en los Juegos Olímpicos - #SombrasEnLosJuegos Cap. 6* [Video]. YouTube. https://www.youtube.com/watch?v=YFIrH867fK8&ab_channel=DEPORTV

Dictionary-Random House Unabridged Dictionary. (2019). *Definition of faith | Dictionary.* dictionary. https://www.dictionary.com/browse/faith

Documentary Central. (2022). *Fighting To End 100 Years Of Woman's Suffrage In The UK | Emmeline Pankhurst | Documentary Central* [Video]. YouTube. https://www.youtube.com/watch?v=OFlPAkl4jr0&ab_channel=DocumentaryCentral

Documentary Central. (2022). *The People's Princess | Diana At 60 | Full Documentary | Documentary Central* [Video]. YouTube. https://www.youtube.com/watch?v=jZkypM1EUJg&ab_channel=DocumentaryCentral

Dr. Jane Goodall & the Jane Goodall Institute USA. (2022). *Storytime with Dr. Jane - With Love: Flo and Flint* [Video]. YouTube. https://www.youtube.com/watch?v=sJ5IPxY6W-U&t=20s&ab_channel=Dr.JaneGoodall%26theJaneGoodallInstituteUSA

Dragos, D. (2015, September 5). *Blog: Neuroscience Shows How Following Your Passion Makes You Happy - Science and Spirituality with Dr Dragos.* Dr Dragos. https://drdragos.com/neuroscience-shows-following-passion-makes-happy/#:~:text=DOPAMINE%3A%20When%20we%20EXPLORE%20and

Drucker, P. (1954). *Management is doing things right, leadership is doing the right things.* Doctor Quote. https://doctor-quote.com/quotes/management-is-doing-things-right-leadership-is-doing-the-right-things/

Editors, Biography. com. (2021, March 26). *Rosa Parks - Quotes, Bus Boycott & Death.* Biography; A&E Television Networks. https://www.biography.com/activists/rosa-parks

Elliott, J. K. (2019, April 27). Why anti-apartheid hero Nelson Mandela was once labelled a terrorist. *Global News.* https://globalnews.ca/news/5201623/nelson-mandela-apartheid-terrorist-south-africa/

En10minutos. (2019). *Clara Schumann en 10 minutos* [Video]. YouTube. https://www.youtube.com/watch?v=IYtx-iPNXQ4&ab_channel=en10minutos

Encyclopaedia Britannica. (2010). *Nora Ephron | Biography, Books, Plays, Movies, & Facts.* https://www.britannica.com/biography/Nora-Ephron

Encyclopedia of Ecology. (2008). *Ecological Resilience - an overview | ScienceDirect Topics.* ScienceDirect. https://www.sciencedirect.com/topics/agricultural-and-biological-sciences/ecological-resilience#:~:text=Ecological%20Resilience-

Engel, K. (2014). *Fe del Mundo, first female student at Harvard Medical School | Amazing Women In History*. Amazing Women in History. https://amazingwom eninhistory.com/fe-del-mundo/

English Oxford Living Dictionaries. (2016, September 25). *faith - definition of faith in English | Oxford Dictionaries*. Web.archive.org. https://web.archive.org/web/20160925102845/https://en.oxforddictionaries.com/definition/faith

English Oxford Living Dictionaries. (2017, May 4). *passion - definition of passion in English | Oxford Dictionaries*. Web.archive.org. https://web.archive.org/web/20170504214510/https:/en.oxforddictionaries.com/definition/passion

Europe 1. (2022). *Alice Milliat rame, rame, rame...* [Video] YouTube. https://www.youtube.com/watch?v=y091socemvc&list=TLPQMDEwMzIwMjPPTuFXYh7 mAQ&index=2&ab_channel=Europe1

Foster, B., & Foster, M. (2002). *The Secret Lives of Alexandra David-Neel: A Biography of the Explorer of Tibet and Its Forbidden Practices*. Overlook Books. https://www.amazon.com/Secret-Lives-Alexandra-David-Neel-Biogra-phy/dp/1585673293

Freeman, P. (2020). Social Support in Sport. *Handbook of Sport Psychology*, 447–463. https://doi.org/10.1002/9781119568124.ch21

Fulker, R. (2019). Clara Schumann: artista y supermujer del siglo XIX – DW. *Deutsche Welle*. https://www.dw.com/es/clara-schumann-artista-y-supermu jer-del-siglo-xix/a-50425190

GBH News. (2016). *Mile 5: Breaking the Mold: The Story of Bobbi Gibb* [Video]. YouTube. https://www.youtube.com/watch?v=2LjGKwedIIU&ab_channel= GBHNews

Gibb, R. (n.d.). *Roberta "Bobbi" Gibb - A Run of One's Own*. Runningpast. http://runningpast.com/gibb_story.htm

Godin, B. (2020, October 29). *Women of Interest—Ruth Bader Ginsburg | The Voice*. Web.archive.org. https://web.archive.org/web/20201029052546/https://www.voicemagazine.org/2020/10/21/women-of-interest-ruth-bader-ginsburg/

Goldsmith, B. (2008). *Obsessive Genius The Inner World of Marie Curie*. Paw Prints. https://www.amazon.com/Obsessive-Genius-Inner-World-Discoveries/dp/0393327485

Golen, J. (2017, April 15). *How running pioneers Kathrine Switzer and Bobbi Gibb outran Boston Marathon tradition*. Boston. https://www.boston.com/sports/boston-marathon/2017/04/15/running-pioneers-kathrine-switzer-bobbi-gibb-took-their-own-paths-to-change/

Goodall, J., & Berman, P. (2000). *Reason for Hope: A Spiritual Journey (Revised ed. edition)*. Grand Central Publishing. https://www.amazon.com/Reason-Hope-Spiritual-Jane-Goodall/dp/0446676136

Goorjian, M. A. (Director). (2007). *Louis Hay - You Can Heal Your Life* [Video]. YouTube. https://www.youtube.com/watch?v=hhDuFLWwGAQ&ab_chan nel=VladimirLatinovic

Gorman, M. (2017, April 16). The Boston Marathon and how Kathrine Switzer's number 261 became a symbol for women in sports. *Newsweek*. https://www. newsweek.com/boston-marathon-kathrine-switzer-261-fearless-symbol-women-running-584645

Graham, J. (n.d.). *Bulletin #4422, Violence Part 2: Shame and Humiliation - Cooperative Extension Publications - University of Maine Cooperative Extension*. Cooperative Extension Publications. Retrieved April 25, 2021, from https://extension. umaine.edu/publications/4422e/

Gyatso, T. (2019). *Compassion and the Individual*. The 14th Dalai Lama. https:// www.dalailama.com/messages/compassion-and-human-values/compassion

Hardon, J. (2000). *Dictionary : INTELLECTUAL VISION*. catholicculture.org. https://www.catholicculture.org/culture/library/dictionary/index.cfm?id= 34262

History Channel. (2018). *Ruth Bader Ginsburg, Brooklyn's Own Supreme Court Justice | History* [Video]. YouTube. https://www.youtube.com/watch?v=Asbju X0YxzY&list=TLPQMjAwMzIwMjP-hX-TGhDVgQ&index=6&ab_channel= HISTORY

Hollings, C., Martin, U., & Rice, A. C. (2018). *Ada Lovelace : the making of a computer scientist*. Bodleian Library. https://www.amazon.com/Ada-Lovelace-Making-Computer-Scientist/dp/1851244883

Hopper, E. (2014, August 8). *By Supporting Others, You Support Yourself: Findings from Social Psychology*. HealthyPsych. https://healthypsych.com/by-support ing-others-you-support-yourself-findings-from-social-psychology/

Horsley, K. (2010). *Florence Nightingale*. Jmvh.org. https://jmvh.org/article/ florence-nightingale/

Horton, R., & Simmons, S. (2006). *Women who changed the world : fifty inspirational women who shaped history*. Quercus. https://www.amazon.com/Women-Who-Changed-World-Inspirational/dp/1847240267

Houck, A. M., & Smentkowski, B. P. (2019). *Ruth Bader Ginsburg*. In Ency-clopædia Britannica. https://www.britannica.com/biography/Ruth-Bader-Ginsburg

Hume, D. (2019). *Treatise Of Human Nature*. Digireads Com. https://www.ama-zon.com/Treatise-Human-Nature-Philosophical-Classics/dp/0486432505 (Original work published 1739)

Hvidt, N. C. (2007). *Christian prophecy : the post-biblical tradition*. Oxford Univer-sity Press. https://www.amazon.com/Christian-Prophecy-Post-Biblical-Niels-Hvidt/dp/0195314476

Insightful & Inspirational Composer Quotes. (n.d.). Buffalo Toronto Public Media. Retrieved June 30, 2023, from https://www.wned.org/blogs/wned-classical-blog/insightful-inspirational-composer-quotes/#:~:text=CLARA%20SCHU MANN%20(1819%2D1896)%3A

Isc. (2021). *The grandmother to a generation - The Astrid Lindgren story* [Video].

YouTube. https://www.youtube.com/watch?v=zlBFfiU2qCE&list=TLPQMjI
wNDIwMjNy-7DXl8XbTw&index=5&ab_channel=Isc

Jenkins, A., Zhu, L., & Hsu, M. (2016). Cognitive neuroscience of honesty and deception: A signaling framework. *Current Opinion in Behavioral Sciences, 11,* 130–137. https://doi.org/10.1016/j.cobeha.2016.09.005

KCTS 9. (2011). *Nora Ephron | CONVERSATIONS AT KCTS 9* [Video]. YouTube. https://www.youtube.com/watch?v=SXiNEgO-wxo&ab_channel=KCTS9

Kelley, L., & Kelley, L. (2015, October 27). How Ruth Bader Ginsburg Became the "Notorious RBG." *Rolling Stone.* https://www.rollingstone.com/culture/culture-features/how-ruth-bader-ginsburg-became-the-notorious-rbg-50388/

King, B. (1921). *The Conquest of Fear.* Wilder Publications. https://www.amazon.com/Conquest-Fear-Basil-King/dp/1617202991

kingsmedicine. (2020). *How Rosalind Franklin changed history* [Video]. YouTube. https://www.youtube.com/watch?v=rjB_OKZK2r4&ab_channel=kingsmedicine

Kirilova, K. (2019, October 10). *How to cope with the unexpected?* Career Life Choices. https://careerlifechoices.com/how-to-cope-with-the-unexpected/

Klein, H. (2017). *The Wild Life of Clara Schumann* [Video]. YouTube. https://www.youtube.com/watch?v=O4k7ioNBp7o&ab_channel=HannahKlein

Lavrín, A., & American Council Of Learned Societies. (1998). *Women, feminism, and social change in Argentina, Chile, and Uruguay, 1890-1940.* University Of Nebraska Press. https://www.worldcat.org/es/title/45729374

Leonard, J. (2020, December 9). *Kathrine Switzer: A Running Pioneer.* Impowerage. https://impowerage.com/kathrine-switzer/

Levine, E., & Munguia Gomez, D. (2020). "I'm just being honest." When and why honesty enables help versus harm. *Journal of Personality and Social Psychology.* https://doi.org/10.1037/pspi0000242

Louise Hay. (n.d.). *About Louise Hay | Bio & Timeline of Achievements.* https://www.louisehay.com/about/#timeline

Lucchetti, A. (2013). Muriel Siebert, Pioneer at NYSE, Dies at 80. *WSJ.* https://www.wsj.com/articles/SB10001424127887323407104579035693004640988

Luther, M. (2019). *Strength to love.* Beacon Press. https://www.amazon.com/Strength-Love-Martin-Luther-King/dp/080705190X (Original work published 1963)

Maddox, B. (2003). The double helix and the "wronged heroine." *Nature, 421*(6921), 407–408. https://doi.org/10.1038/nature01399

Mahmood, Z. (2018, March 8). Bones from Pacific island likely those of Amelia Earhart, researchers say. *CNN.* https://edition.cnn.com/2018/03/08/health/amelia-earhart-bones-island-intl/index.html

Makers. (2013). *Muriel Siebert: First Lady of Wall Street* [Video]. YouTube. https://www.youtube.com/watch?v=Izx0NAD45gc&ab_channel=MAKERS

Malti, T. (2020). Kindness: a perspective from developmental psychology.

European Journal of Developmental Psychology, 1–29. https://doi.org/10.1080/17405629.2020.1837617

Marino, K. M. (2013). *LA VANGUARDIA FEMINISTA: PAN-AMERICAN FEMINISM AND THE RISE OF INTERNATIONAL WOMEN'S RIGHTS, 1915-1946.* https://stacks.stanford.edu/file/druid:nj335cm4420/Marino%20Dissertation-augmented.pdf

Marino, K. M. (2019). *Feminism for the Americas : the making of an international human rights movement.* The University of North Carolina Press. https://www.worldcat.org/es/title/1043051115

Mark, C. (2018, September 17). The psychological secret to turning your next failure into success. *CBC.* https://www.cbc.ca/life/wellness/the-psychological-secret-to-turning-your-next-failure-into-success-1.4827346

Markman, A. (2021, April 21). *People Can Use Honesty to Justify Selfishness | Psychology Today.* psychologytoday. https://www.psychologytoday.com/intl/blog/ulterior-motives/202104/people-can-use-honesty-justify-selfishness

Mascolo de Filippis, J., & de Maximy, A. (1993). *Alexandra David Neel, du Sikkim au Tibet interdit* [Video]. YouTube. https://www.youtube.com/watch?v=8YAODcV4IuY&ab_channel=MelodyNelson

Merriam-Webster. (2009a). *Definition of compassion.* Merriam-Webster. https://www.merriam-webster.com/dictionary/compassion

Merriam-Webster. (2009b). *Definition of COURAGE.* Merriam-Webster. https://www.merriam-webster.com/dictionary/courage

Merriam-Webster. (2011). *Definition of FAITH.* Merriam-Webster. https://www.merriam-webster.com/dictionary/faith

Merriam-Webster. (2018). *Definition of SUPPORT.* Merriam-Webster. https://www.merriam-webster.com/dictionary/support

Merriam-Webster. (2019a). *Definition of BELIEF.* Merriam-Webster. https://www.merriam-webster.com/dictionary/belief

Merriam-Webster. (2019b). *Definition of FAILURE.* Merriam-Webster. https://www.merriam-webster.com/dictionary/failure

Merriam-Webster. (2019c). *Definition of HONESTY.* Merriam-Webster. https://www.merriam-webster.com/dictionary/honesty

Merriam-Webster. (2019d). *Definition of KINDNESS.* Merriam-Webster. https://www.merriam-webster.com/dictionary/kindness

Merriam-Webster. (2019e). *Definition of passion.* Merriam-Webster. https://www.merriam-webster.com/dictionary/passion

Merriam-Webster. (2019f). *Definition of PERSEVERANCE.* Merriam-Webster. https://www.merriam-webster.com/dictionary/perseverance

Merriam-Webster. (2019g). *Definition of SETBACK.* Merriam-Webster. https://www.merriam-webster.com/dictionary/setback

Merriam-Webster. (2019h). *Definition of VISION.* Merriam-Webster. https://www.merriam-webster.com/dictionary/vision

Merriam-Webster. (2019i). *Definition of VULNERABILITY*. Merriam-Webster. https://www.merriam-webster.com/dictionary/vulnerability

Merriam-Webster. (n.d.-a). *Definition of DIRECTION*. Merriam-Webster. https://www.merriam-webster.com/dictionary/direction

Merriam-Webster. (n.d.-b). *Definition of EXPECT*. Merriam-Webster. https://www.merriam-webster.com/dictionary/expect

Merriam-Webster. (n.d.-c). *Definition of PERSISTENCE*. Merriam-Webster. https://www.merriam-webster.com/dictionary/persistence

Merriam-Webster. (n.d.-d). *Definition of RESILIENCE*. Merriam-Webster. https://www.merriam-webster.com/dictionary/resilience#:~:text=In%20physics%2C%20resilience%20is%20the

Middleton, R. (1989). *Alexandra David-Neel: Portait of an Adventurer*. Shambhala. https://www.amazon.com/Alexandra-David-Neel-Adventurer-Ruth-Middleton/dp/0877734135

Milde, H. (2014, March 8). *Kathrine Switzer and Roger Robinson visit the Berlin Sports Museum - AIMS Marathon Museum of Running - An icon of the marathon and running scene finds her history. A report by Horst*. German Road Races. Web.archive.org. https://web.archive.org/web/20140308220723/http://www.germanroadraces.de/274-1-16454-kathrine-switzer-and-roger-robinson-visit-the.html

Mitchell, S. (1977). Women's Participation in the Olympic Games 1900-1926. *Journal of Sport History*, *4*(2), 208–228. https://www.jstor.org/stable/43609254?read-now=1&oauth_data=eyJlbWFpbCI6Im0uY291c3Npcm0FOQGdtYWlsLmNvbSIsImluc3RpdHV0aW9uIjpbXX0&seq=5

Montanari, F. (2014). *The Brill Dictionary of Ancient Greek Online (M. Goh & C. Schroeder, Eds.)*. Brill. https://brill.com/display/db/bdgo

Moore, C. (2013). *Margaret Thatcher : the authorized biography, Volume Three: Herself Alone*. Allen Lane. https://www.amazon.com/Margaret-Thatcher-Authorized-Biography-Herself/dp/0241324742

Morales, R. (n.d.). *Bessie Coleman*. Sites.rootsweb. https://sites.rootsweb.com/~txecm/bessie_coleman.htm

Morton, A., & Internet Archive. (1997). *Diana : her true story- in her own words*. Simon & Schuster. https://archive.org/details/dianahertruestor00mort

Munguia Gomez, D. M. (2021). *Research – David M. Munguia Gomez*. David M. Munguia Gomez. https://www.davidmunguiagomez.com/research/

National Geographic Society. (2019). *Jane Goodall*. Nationalgeographic.org. https://www.nationalgeographic.org/education/channel/jane-goodall/

National Library of Medicine. (2019, March 12). *Biographical Overview*. Rosalind Franklin - Profiles in Science. https://profiles.nlm.nih.gov/spotlight/kr/feature/biographical

Natural Resources Conservation Service Nevada. (2015). *Women in History | NRCS Nevada*. Archive.org. https://web.archive.org/web/20160216203428/http://www.nrcs.usda.gov/wps/portal/nrcs/detail/nv/about/?cid=nrcs144p2_037528

Neff, K. D. (2009). The Role of Self-Compassion in Development: A Healthier Way to Relate to Oneself. *Human Development*, 52(4), 211–214. https://doi.org/10.1159/000215071

Neff, K. D., Rude, S. S., & Kirkpatrick, K. L. (2007). An examination of self-compassion in relation to positive psychological functioning and personality traits. *Journal of Research in Personality*, 41(4), 908–916. https://doi.org/10.1016/j.jrp.2006.08.002

New Advent. (2021). *CATHOLIC ENCYCLOPEDIA: Visions and Apparitions*. newadvent.org. https://www.newadvent.org/cathen/15477a.htm

NowThis Originals. (2023). *Breaking Barriers: Muriel Siebert's Inspiring Journey as "First Woman of Finance"* [Video]. YouTube. https://www.youtube.com/watch?v=QXCHbiPfzIU&ab_channel=NowThisOriginals

Olsthoorn, P. (2007). Courage in the Military: Physical and Moral. *Journal of Military Ethics*, 6(4), 270–279. https://doi.org/10.1080/15027570701755471

Online Etymology Dictionary. (n.d.). *compassion | Search Online Etymology Dictionary*. etymonline. https://www.etymonline.com/search?q=compassion

Oppenheimer, M. (2008, May 4). The Queen of the New Age. *The New York Times*. https://www.nytimes.com/2008/05/04/magazine/04Hay-t.html

Osborne, L. (2019, December 7). Prince Andrew and Jeffrey Epstein: what you need to know. *The Guardian*. https://www.theguardian.com/uk-news/2019/dec/07/prince-andrew-jeffrey-epstein-what-you-need-to-know

Osorio, C. (2021, March 7). Paulina Luisi, la médica pionera que luchó por el derecho al voto de las mujeres. *El País*. https://elpais.com/internacional/2021-03-07/paulina-luisi-la-medica-pionera-que-lucho-por-el-derecho-al-voto-de-las-mujeres.html

Oxford Languages. (2010). *Oxford Dictionary of English*. Oxford University Press. https://www.amazon.com/-/es/Oxford-Languages/dp/0199571120/ref=sr_1_1?keywords=9780199571123&linkCode=qs&qid=1688008802&s=books&sr=1-1

Oxford University Press. (1968). *Oxford Latin dictionary*. Oxford University Press. https://archive.org/details/aa.-vv.-oxford-latin-dictionary-1968

Oxford University Press. (1999). *The Oxford American dictionary and language guide*. Oxford University Press. https://www.amazon.com/Oxford-American-Dictionary-Language-Guide/dp/0195134494

Pankhurst, E. (1914). *My own Story*. London Nash. https://books.google.co.za/books?id=LgkxAQAAMAAJ&printsec=frontcover&dq=Emmeline+Pankhurst&hl=en&sa=X&redir_esc=y

Parks, R., & Haskins, J. (1999). *Rosa Parks : My Story*. Puffin Books. https://www.amazon.com/Rosa-Parks-My-Story/dp/0141301201

Pearce, J. (2019, August 15). *To Live Your Truth, Start by Being Honest with Yourself*. GoodTherapy.org Therapy Blog. https://www.goodtherapy.org/blog/to-live-your-truth-start-by-being-honest-with-yourself-0815194

Peck, H. T. (1898). *Harry Thurston Peck, Harpers Dictionary of Classical Antiquities*

(1898), F, Felix, Fides. In perseus.tufts.edu. Harper and Brothers. https://www.
perseus.tufts.edu/hopper/text?doc=Perseus%3Atext%3A1999.04.0062%3Aal
phabetic+letter%3DF%3Aentry+group%3D3%3Aentry%3Dfides2-harpers

Peterson, D. (2008). *Jane Goodall : the woman who redefined man.* Mariner Books.
https://www.amazon.com/Jane-Goodall-Woman-Who-
Redefined/dp/0547053568

Physiopedia. (n.d.). *Personal Values and Beliefs.* https://www.physio-pedia.com/
Personal_Values_and_Beliefs#cite_note-:0-1

Pianalto, M. (2012). Moral Courage and Facing Others. *International Journal of
Philosophical Studies, 20*(2), 165–184. https://doi.org/10.1080/09672559.
2012.668308

Pirani, F. (2018). Who was Fe del Mundo? Google honors Filipina doctor, first
woman admitted to Harvard Medical School. *Ajc.* https://www.ajc.com/
news/world/who-was-del-mundo-google-honors-filipino-doctor-first-
woman-admitted-harvard-medical-school/oStEMNmKc5KEz27R9X4etN/

Psychologs Magazine. (2019, December 18). Psychology of Failure life. https://
www.psychologs.com/psychology-of-failure-life/

Psychology IResearchNet. (2016, January 11). *Social Support - IResearchNet.*
Psychology. http://psychology.iresearchnet.com/social-psychology/interper
sonal-relationships/social-support/

Putman, D. (2001). The Emotions of Courage. *Journal of Social Philosophy, 32*(4),
463–470. https://doi.org/10.1111/0047-2786.00107

Random Acts of Kindness Foundation. (2019). *Random Acts of Kindness.* https://
www.randomactsofkindness.org/

Redniss, L. (2010). *Radioactive : Marie & Pierre Curie : a tale of love & fallout.* It
Books. https://www.amazon.com/Radioactive-Marie-Pierre-Curie-Fall-
out/dp/0061351326

Reich, N. B. (2001). *Clara Schumann, the artist and the woman.* Cornell University
Press. https://www.amazon.com/Clara-Schumann-Nancy-B-
Reich/dp/0801486378

Reitan, E. A., Thatcher, M., Major, J., & Blair, T. (2003). *The Thatcher revolution :
Margaret Thatcher, John Major, and Tony Blair, 1979-2001.* Rowman & Littlefield,
Cop. https://books.google.com.ar/books/about/The_Thatcher_Revolu-
tion.html?id=7qaMqwGRE00C&redir_esc=y

Rogers, S. (1955). *Rosa Parks Interview* [Video]. https://www.youtube.com/
watch?v=28CExaXv7aA&ab_channel=AfroMarxist

Roosevelt, E. (1937). *This is My Story.* Harper & Brothers. https://www.amazon.-
com/This-My-Story-Eleanor-Roosevelt/dp/B0006ANWHM

Royal College of Nursing Wales. (2022). *RCN Wales Betsi Cadwaladr Biennial
Lecture 2022* [Video]. YouTube. https://www.youtube.com/watch?v=hj3QF
PmLrG0&list=TLPQMzAwMzIwMjIwMjOFLVypJrxTXw&index=2&ab_channel=
RCNWales

RT Documentary. (2016). *Valentina Tereshkova: Seagull in Space* [Video]. YouTube. https://www.youtube.com/watch?v=V4rN9kge3rg&list=TLPQMDYwMjIw MjMfzDOjc1vSig&index=6&ab_channel=usarussia

Ruiz-Grossman, S. (2021, October 13). Katie Couric Edited Out Controversial Comments By RBG On Kneeling Protests: Book. *HuffPost*. https://www.huff post.com/entry/katie-couric-book-ruth-bader-ginsburg-kneeling-protests_n_616755e8e4b065a5496f7184

Sagiv, L., & Schwartz, S. H. (2021). Personal Values Across Cultures. *Annual Review of Psychology, 73*(1). https://doi.org/10.1146/annurev-psych-020821-125100

Saiegh, D. (2022). *Paulina Luisi, la primera feminista uruguaya | Las Incansables* [Video]. YouTube. https://www.youtube.com/watch?v=1pV65XaWICg& list=TLPQMDgwNDIwMjMOfcb6EuGKKg&index=3&ab_channel= DanilaSaiegh

Salaverria, L. B. (2011, August 7). Beautiful life as doctor to generations of kids; 99. *INQUIRER.net*. https://newsinfo.inquirer.net/37419/beautiful-life-as-doctor-to-generations-of-kids-99

Sandage, S. A. (2005). *Born losers : a history of failure in America*. Harvard University Press. https://www.amazon.com/Born-Losers-History-Failure-America-ebook/dp/B002JCSCP2

Sapriza, G. (2011). *Paulina Luisi. Liderazgo, alianzas y desencuentros de las sufragistas | 1811-2011*. 1811-2011.Edu.uy. http://www.1811-2011.edu.uy/B1/content/ paulina-luisi-liderazgo-alianzas-y-desencuentros-de-las-sufragistas? page=show

Sapriza, G. (2020). *Ciencia y Reforma Social Paulina Luisi: Esperanzas y Dilemas de la Primera Médica Del Uruguay*. YouTube; Academia Nacional de Medicina. https://www.youtube.com/watch?v=Wf89x4mSC-8&list=TLPQMDgwNDI wMjMOfcb6EuGKKg&index=5&ab_channel=ANMUruguay

Schaffner, A. K. (2020, September 16). *Perseverance in Psychology: Meaning, Importance & Books*. PositivePsychology. https://positivepsychology.com/persever ance/#:~:text=Perseverance%20refers%20to%20our%20ability

Scholarly Community Encyclopedia. (2022). *Courage*. Encyclopedia.pub. https:// encyclopedia.pub/entry/31768

Schwitzgebel, E. (2019). *Belief (E. N. Zalta, Ed.)*. Stanford Encyclopedia of Philosophy; Metaphysics Research Lab, Stanford University. https://plato.stanford. edu/entries/belief/#Bib

Science Museum. (2015). *The first woman in space* [Video]. YouTube. https://www. youtube.com/watch?v=jmW2eUlrmw8&ab_channel=ScienceMuseum

Selanders, L. (2018). *Florence Nightingale | Biography & Facts*. In Encyclopædia Britannica. https://www.britannica.com/biography/Florence-Nightingale

Siebert, M., & Ball, A. L. (2002). *Changing the Rules: Adventures of a Wall Street Maverick*. Free Press. https://www.amazon.com/-/es/Muriel-

Siebert/dp/0743211146/ref=sr_1_1?keywords=9780743211147&link-Code=qs&qid=1688627774&s=books&sr=1-1

Slotnik, D. E. (2019, December 11). Overlooked No More: Bessie Coleman, Pioneering African-American Aviatrix. *The New York Times.* https://www.nytimes.com/2019/12/11/obituaries/bessie-coleman-overlooked.html

Spragg Nilsson, T. (2019). *Do you know Astrid Lindgren? | #BecomingSwedish* [Video]. YouTube. https://www.youtube.com/watch?v=268VdXiSoFk&list=TLPQMjIwNDIwMjNy-7DXl8XbTw&index=6&ab_channel=TomasSpraggNilsson

Stanborough, R. J. (2020, July 23). Fear of the Unknown: Causes, Symptoms, Risk Factors, & Treatment. *Healthline.* https://www.healthline.com/health/understanding-and-overcoming-fear-of-the-unknown

Stasiak, A. (2003). The first lady of DNA. *EMBO Reports, 4*(1), 14. https://doi.org/10.1038/sj.embor.embor723

Strachey, L. (1918). *Eminent Victorians.* Chatto And Windus London. https://archive.org/details/in.ernet.dli.2015.225424

Strauss, C., Lever Taylor, B., Gu, J., Kuyken, W., Baer, R., Jones, F., & Cavanagh, K. (2016). What is compassion and how can we measure it? A review of definitions and measures. *Clinical Psychology Review, 47*(47), 15–27. https://doi.org/10.1016/j.cpr.2016.05.004

Swafford, J. (2003, April 26). Bittersweet symphonies. *The Guardian.* https://www.theguardian.com/music/2003/apr/26/classicalmusicandopera.artsfeatures2

Swenson, K., & Missouri University Press. (2005). *Medical women and Victorian fiction.* Columbia : University of Missouri Press. https://archive.org/details/medicalwomenvict00swen_0/page/n5/mode/2up

Team Tonny. (2021, February 18). *How to be honest with yourself | Tony Robbins.* Tonyrobbins. https://www.tonyrobbins.com/mind-meaning/be-honest-with-yourself/

TED-Ed. (2016). *Rosalind Franklin: DNA's unsung hero - Cláudio L. Guerra* [Video]. YouTube. https://www.youtube.com/watch?v=BIP0lYrdirI&list=TLPQMTIwNDIwMjNyHrRjIFOsxw&index=5&ab_channel=TED-Ed

The 92nd Street Y, New York. (2019). *Supreme Court Justice Ruth Bader Ginsburg with David Rubenstein* [Video]. YouTube. https://www.youtube.com/watch?v=0bZZiy16pu4&ab_channel=The92ndStreetY%2CNewYork

The Guardian. (2018, May 10). Margaret Thatcher: a life in quotes. https://www.theguardian.com/politics/2013/apr/08/margaret-thatcher-quotes

The History Chicks. (2019, December 9). *Episode 141: Rosa Parks Revisited.* https://thehistorychicks.com/episode-141-rosa-parks-revisited/

The National Art Museum of Sport. (2012, May 7). *placeholder | NAMOS · The National Art Museum of Sport.* Web.archive.org. https://web.archive.org/web/20120507102749/http://www.namos.iupui.edu/artists/Artist.aspx?artist=167

The New York Times. (1967). Lady With Desire to Run Crashed Marathon. Archive.org. https://web.archive.org/web/20120306124858/http://www.mediaed.org/assets/products/151/Kathy_Switzer.pdf

The People Profiles. (2021). *Eleanor Roosevelt - The Greatest First Lady? Documentary* [Video]. YouTube. https://www.youtube.com/watch?v=IlqJaJuEvds&ab_channel=ThePeopleProfiles

The South African College of Applied Psychology. (2016, November 7). *Understanding the Psychology of Failure*. SACAP. https://www.sacap.edu.za/blog/applied-psychology/the-psychology-of-failure/

The University of Alabama at Birmingham. (2011). *UAB - Libraries - The Life of Florence Nightingale*. Uab.edu. https://library.uab.edu/locations/reynolds/collections/florence-nightingale/life

Theroux, M. (2020, June 14). Alexandra David-Néel, the first European woman to see Lhasa. *The Guardian*. https://www.theguardian.com/travel/2020/jun/14/explorer-alexandra-david-neel-first-western-woman-lhasa-tibet

Tirel, M. (2020, March 26). *Self-Honesty: Examples Of Why It's So Important (+ Studies)*. Tracking Happiness. https://www.trackinghappiness.com/self-honesty-examples/

True Story Documentary Channel. (2022). *Discovering Coco Chanel - True Story Documentary Channel* [Video]. YouTube. https://www.youtube.com/watch?v=ZqO8Iw1lLVM&list=TLPQMjgwMTIwMjOoGagOP7KcyQ&index=7&ab_channel=TrueStoryDocumentaryChannel

Underhill, E. (2002). *Mysticism a Study in the Natureand Development of Spiritual Consciousness*. Dover Publications. https://www.amazon.com/Mysticism-Nature-Development-Spiritual-Consciousness/dp/0486422380

UNICEF. (2018). *Gender equality*. https://www.unicef.org/gender-equality

United Nations. (2022). *Gender equality and women's empowerment*. United Nations Sustainable Development. https://www.un.org/sustainabledevelopment/gender-equality/

Uribarri, R. (2021). Alice Milliat: la madre del deporte olímpico femenino. *Ctxt.es | Contexto Y Acción*. https://ctxt.es/es/20211101/Deportes/37834/mujeres-juegos-olimpicos-alice-milliat-ricardo-uribarri.htm

Vaish, A., Grossmann, T., & Woodward, A. (2008). Not all emotions are created equal: The negativity bias in social-emotional development. *Psychological Bulletin, 134*(3), 383–403. https://doi.org/10.1037/0033-2909.134.3.383

Van Pelt, L. (2006). *Amelia Earhart*. Forge Books. https://www.amazon.com/Amelia-Earhart-Limit-American-Heroes/dp/0765310619

Vaughan, H. (2012). *Sleeping with the enemy : Coco Chanel's secret war*. Vintage Books. https://www.amazon.com/Sleeping-Enemy-Coco-Chanels-Secret/dp/0307475913

Washington Post. (2020). *Ruth Bader Ginsburg's life, in her own words* [Video]. YouTube. https://www.youtube.com/watch?v=7lXhw0LKo-Q&list=TLPQMjAwMzIwMjP-hX-TGhDVgQ&index=4&ab_channel=WashingtonPost

WatchMojo. (2011). *Margaret Thatcher: Biography of the Iron Lady* [Video].. YouTube. https://www.youtube.com/watch?v=rwGV2Kle9EI&list= TLPQMTcwMzIwMjNXthk01RElAQ&index=2&ab_channel= WatchMojo.com

Watson, K. M. (2013, April 29). *Wesley Didn't Say It: Do all the good you can, by all the means you can....* Kevin M. Watson. https://kevinmwatson.com/2013/04/ 29/wesley-didnt-say-it-do-all-the-good-you-can-by-all-the-means-you-can/

Wikipedia. (2001, January 15). *Wikipedia.* Wikipedia.org; Wikimedia Foundation. https://www.wikipedia.org/

Williams, J. (2012, June 27). *Nora Ephron, the Queen of Quips.* ArtsBeat. https:// archive.nytimes.com/artsbeat.blogs.nytimes.com/2012/06/27/nora-ephron-the-queen-of-quips/?action=click&module=RelatedCoverage&pgtype=Arti cle&region=Footer

Yanes, J., & Ventana al Conocimiento. (2015, December 9). *Ada Lovelace: Original and Visionary, but No Programmer.* OpenMind. https://www.bbvaopenmind. com/en/technology/visionaries/ada-lovelace-original-and-visionary-but-no-programmer/

Yarnhub. (2019). *The life and disappearance of Amelia Earhart* [Video]. YouTube. https://www.youtube.com/watch?v=SITeCEuxZII&ab_channel=Yarnhub

Yeung, J. W. K., Zhang, Z., & Kim, T. Y. (2018). Volunteering and health benefits in general adults: cumulative effects and forms. *BMC Public Health, 18*(1). https://doi.org/10.1186/s12889-017-4561-8

Zainal, N. H., & Newman, M. G. (2019). Relation between cognitive and behavioral strategies and future change in common mental health problems across 18 years. *Journal of Abnormal Psychology, 128*(4), 295–304. https://doi.org/10. 1037/abn0000428

ACKNOWLEDGMENTS

Like most books, many people were involved at some stage of this book's journey. I am immensely grateful for the wonderful souls who have supported me in finalizing these lines. Thank you, Rebecca, Nadine, Artemis, Marianne, Frankie, Ali, Sophie, Virginie, CJ, Hayley and Lauren, for being a guide, friend, expert, support, critic and inspiration. Thank you for sharing laughter and tears along the way.

To my mentors over the years: Anni and Gunther, Uli, Hans-Christoph, Elizabeth, Jackie, Fiona, Suchita, Lara, Charles, Jennifer and Mary.

To my family, supporting my late nights at the computer and – consequently – tolerating countless tired mornings. To my dad, who left this world far too early, dedicated to supporting others, and raised me to grow strong and kind. To the incredible women in my family: Marga, Sophie, Greta, Helga, Elke and Ellen.

I am deeply grateful for all the blessings in my life, especially the blessings in disguise. Without them, this book would have never happened.

To all the amazing women past and present, who make this world a better place.

ABOUT THE AUTHOR

Dr Katja Lindemann MD, started her medical career initially in nursing 30 years ago and has spent the last two decades working as a medical doctor and Specialist in Paediatric Psychiatry in various countries.

She deeply cares about different cultures and the importance of inclusion and respect for elders. Her experiences with life challenges and adversity have led her to emphasize the value of connectedness within families and communities.

Residing in the tranquil countryside of southern Australia, she continues to make a difference in the lives of vulnerable young people and their families. Her unwavering dedication to her patients and her passionate advocacy for their well-being is truly inspiring.

Throughout her career, she has also taken on other top-level positions in a primarily male-dominated industry. She is focused on supporting and mentoring other women facing similar challenges. Her website, www.katjalindemann.com is an excellent resource for those looking to learn more about her work and connect with her.